not
just
race,
not
just
gender

not just race, not just gender

BLACK FEMINIST READINGS

VALERIE SMITH

Routledge
New York and London

▲ ▲ ▲ ▲ ◆

Published in 1998 by
Routledge
29 West 35th Street
New York, NY 10001

Published in Great Britain by
Routledge
11 New Fetter Lane
London EC4P 4EE

A version of chapter one was first published as "Split Affinities: The Case of Interracial Rape," in *Conflicts in Feminism* (New York: Routledge, 1990). Chapter two first appeared as "Reading the Intersection of Race and Gender in Narratives of Passing," in *Diacritics* 24 (1994), published by Johns Hopkins University Press. Both these chapters have been revised for this book.

Library of Congress Cataloging-in-Publication Data

Smith, Valerie, 1956–
    Not just race, not just gender : Black feminist readings / Valerie Smith.
        p.   cm.
    Includes bibliographical references and index.
    ISBN 0-415-90325-4. — ISBN 0-415-90326-2 (pbk.)
    1. Afro-American women in motion pictures. 2. Afro-Americans in motion pictures. 3. Afro-Americans in literature. 4. Afro-Americans—Social Conditions. 5. Afro-American women in literature. 6. Afro-Americans in literature.   I. Title.
PN1995.9.N4S62   1998
791.43'652042'08996073 — dc21   97-32082
                                                                 CIP

▲ ▲ ▲ ▲ ▲

Contents

▲▲▲▲▲

Acknowledgments

I have been blessed with many kinds of support during the period in which I researched and wrote this book. I am grateful to William Germano of Routledge Press for his wise counsel; his patience and advice helped bring this project to fruition. The National Endowment for the Humanities and the University of California President's Fellowships in the Humanities provided me with fellowships in the early stages of the project. The University of California Humanities Research Institute—especially the members of the Minority Discourse Project—offered me the opportunity to enjoy a year-long, challenging, intellectual exchange. For their helpful suggestions during that period, I particularly wish to thank Lindon Barrett, Alycee Lane, George Lipsitz, Marcyliena Morgan, Kobena Mercer, then-director Mark Rose, and Hertha Wong.

Many friends and colleagues read or listened to different portions of this book; for their insightful responses I thank Elizabeth Abel, Kimberlé Crenshaw, Emory Elliott, Farah Jasmine Griffin, Marianne Hirsch, Margaret Homans, Barbara Johnson, Wahneema Lubiano, Anne K. Mellor, Patricia Parker, Clarence Walker, and Tilly Warnock. Charlotte Pierce-Baker, Houston Baker, Camille Billops, Abena Busia, the late Daniel Calder, Helen Deutsch, Lynell George, Cheryl Harris, Marianne Hirsch, King-kok Cheung, James V. Hatch, Nicole King, Arthur Little, the late Marlon Riggs, Judith Rosen, Sonia Saldivar-Hull, Greg Sarris, the late James Snead, Eric Sundquist, Susan Strasser, David Van Leer, Cheryl Wall, Mary Helen Washington, and Richard Yarborough have nurtured my mind as well as my spirit. I thank each of them for the gifts of friendship and intellectual companionship. The example of their hard work was my principal source of inspiration. I am particularly grateful to David Van Leer for his encouragement and suggestions when I needed them most.

Daphne Brooks, Joni Jones, Ryan Kernan, Keidra Morris, La' Tonya Miles, Connie Razza, Kimberly Slaughter-White, Lisa Thompson, and most especially Sonnet Retman provided me with great conversation as well as insightful and conscientious research assistance. I thank them for their dedication, inspiration, friendship, and love.

I have been fortunate to have had an extensive community of friends whose prayers and faith and prodding sustained me as I wrote this book. Special thanks to the Revs. Makungu Akinyela, Betty Hanna-Witherspoon, Joyce Johnson, Fran Richardson, and Judi Wortham-Sauls; Rita Rothman, Hattie Kilgore, and Eloise Streator.

▲ ▲ ▲ ▲ ▲

Ron Murphy and Dakota came to occupy an important place in my life as this project neared completion. Their companionship, encouragement, and affection helped me immeasurably and I will always be grateful to them both. My family—Will and Josephine, Daryl, Vera, Glenn, Laurie, and Alison—continues to love and believe in me despite everything. Thanks to all of you once again.

Preface

black feminist thinking has always assumed that race and gender are mutually dependent, interlocking cultural constructions and projections. From the nineteenth-century articulations of Sojourner Truth,[1] Harriet Jacobs, and Anna Julia Cooper, to contemporary scholarship in diverse fields including (but not limited to) literary criticism and theory, history, critical race theory, religious studies, anthropology, sociology, and the history of science, black feminists have asserted that ideologies of race, gender (and more recently, class and sexuality) are reciprocally constitutive categories of experience and analysis. To describe the interactions of race and gender as they shape lives and social practices, Kimberlé Crenshaw has coined the term "intersectionality."[2]

Out of the apparent consensus around this assumption has come a multiplicity of intellectual, cultural, and activist work too rich and varied to detail in its entirety here. Some scholars have explored how the presumptive maleness of, say, African-American or American studies (and institutions) and the presumptive whiteness of feminist studies (and institutions) have suppressed black women's experiences, thereby limiting our understanding of certain models of cultural and historical study and analysis. Their work inscribes black women's contributions centrally in cultural contexts and scholarly traditions that had previously marginalized them. Additionally, such studies re-conceptualize those contexts and traditions in light of black women's lives and achievements.

Corresponding work among literary critics and theorists likewise revises the way we understand genres, periodization, and paradigms. These projects bring unacknowledged black women's texts to popular and critical attention and illuminate the subtleties of understudied works. Centering on black women and seeking out their contributions to extra-literary genres (music, performance, oratory, visual culture, and so on), they challenge prevailing narrative conventions and constructions of cultural and literary histories and traditions. Moreover, they question the ability of master narratives to explain discourses and identities marked with the historically constructed meanings of subordinated race, sexual, gender, and class positions.

This book takes up the underlying premise of black feminist thinking to explore what it means to deploy intersectionality as a mode of cultural or textual analysis, what it means to read at the intersections of constructions of race, gender, class, and sexuality. Each chapter focuses on a site that might seem to engage one category of experience—race, class, sex, or gender—over and above the others. In each instance, I explore how the ostensible dominance of one category masks both the operation of the others and the interconnections among them.

For my purposes here, black feminism is not a biologically grounded positionality. Several of the works I discuss were written or directed by African-American women, but the book is not concerned exclusively with black women's cultural production. Some sections address questions of representation in mainstream Hollywood pictures directed by black or white men. Likewise, while certain discussions focus on the interactions of race, class, and womanhood, in others I consider how ideas of masculinity are shaped in relation to ideologies of race and class.[3]

Rather than centering on black women's experiences as such, I argue that black feminism provides strategies of reading simultaneity.[4] I take as a given that black feminist inquiry is a site of critique that challenges monolithic notions of Americanness, womanhood, blackness, or, for that matter, black womanhood. Throughout the book, I use the practice of reading intersectionally to question the implications of ideological and aesthetic liminality. And drawing on the work of cultural studies theorists such as Stuart Hall, Hazel Carby, Wahneema Lubiano, and Kobena Mercer, I assume that identities are discursively produced and never fixed, always involving negotiations of gender, sexuality, race, and class.

The notion of black feminism I explore in this book grows out of an argument I advanced in an earlier essay, one that situates my work within an ongoing debate about the place of black women's experience in black feminism.[5] In "Black Feminist Theory and the Representation of the 'Other,'" I detach black feminist theorizing from the positionality of the critic by treating it as a practice of "reading inscriptions of race ... gender ... and class in modes of cultural expression."[6] This position departs from Barbara Smith's assertion in her pathbreaking article,

"Toward a Black Feminist Criticism," that a body of shared experiences exists that shapes black women's language, literary and critical practices.[7] Likewise, it differs from Patricia Hill Collins's articulation of a specific standpoint theory, based in black women's experiences of struggle and resistance, out of which an intellectual tradition has developed.[8] It is closer, however, to Hazel Carby's and Ann duCille's skepticism of such constructions. For Carby challenges Smith's position, arguing that "a black feminist criticism cannot afford to be essentialist and ahistorical, reducing the experience of all black women to a common denominator and limiting black feminist critics to an exposition of an equivalent black 'female imagination.'" And duCille suggests that designating any experience as distinctly black denies the existence and validity of other modes of black life.[9]

By identifying black feminist theorizing principally as a strategy of reading, I might appear to some readers to have rendered the black feminist invisible. (Indeed, on at least one occasion I have been asked where the black or the feminist is in this project, given that my use of the term requires neither that the reader be a black woman, nor that black women figure in the text under scrutiny.) But I believe that there can be no black feminism without intersectionality, and that, furthermore, the centrality of black women neither indicates nor guarantees a text's ideological commitments. In Stuart Hall's words, "We are always in negotiation, not with a single set of oppositions that place us always in the same relation to others, but with a series of different positionalities."[10] Thus, I read intersectionally in the service of an anti-racist and feminist politics which holds that the power relations that dominate others are complicit in the subordination of black and other women of color as well. Social transformation will become possible only as we understand how these dynamics and relations are inscribed and produced. As Joan Scott aptly argues:

▲ ▲ ▲ ▲ ▲

> The project of making experience visible precludes crit-
> ical examination of the workings of the ideological sys-
> tem itself, its categories of representation (homosexu-
> al/heterosexual, man/woman, black/white as fixed
> immutable identities), its premises about what these cat-
> egories mean and how they operate, and of notions of
> subjects, origin, and cause.[11]

In shifting the focus of my attention from black women's
experiences as such I seek not to privilege undecidability and
ambiguity at the expense of historical specificity. To do so would
deny black women's historical and cultural significance and pre-
clude the possibility of social change. While I want to avoid
notions of identity that are timeless, transparent, or unproblematic in favor of those that are, in Stuart Hall's words, "never
complete, always in process, and always constituted within, not
outside, representation,"[12] I also acknowledge the strategic need
to claim racial, gendered, sexual, and class identities as mean-
ingful in specific ways in the name of struggle and resistance to
institutional violence and exploitation.[13] I simply argue here for
making explicit the contingencies, differences, and discontinu-
ities upon which identities and consensus depend.

Furthermore, I resist deploying what feels like a uniform
model of black women's lived experience because, to my mind,
such models undermine the goals of black feminism in its own
name. If we assume that race, gender, class, and sexuality are
mutually constitutive, and therefore pre-empt ideas of a homo-
geneous women's or black experience, then it should only follow that those constructions also act upon each other within the
category of black women itself, thus problematizing easy gener-
alizations about black women's lives and texts as well.

Until recently, I might have argued that this kind of material-
ist reading, drawing as it does on postmodern conceptions of

subjectivity, represents the logical next step in the development of black feminism, after reactive critique and recuperative, literary archaeological projects. But just as I take issue with essentialist notions of black womanhood, I equally resist attempts to map black feminism along a linear trajectory. A linear, ameliorative model of black feminist analysis runs counter to the critique of "single-axis" frameworks that underlies intersectional modes of interpretation. Moreover, black feminist discourses speak to multiple audiences simultaneously and across history; for some audiences and moments, the certainties of stable notions of identity and community perform more useful ideological work than does the free play of subjectivities posited within cultural studies.

It seems to me that while the rise of poststructuralist theoretical frameworks is certainly in evidence, it is not the only new direction. Equally important are the critique of discursive boundaries and the self-conscious reassessments that allow literary history, oratory, and even autobiography to function as theory. Rather than reading black feminism as an evolution from reactive critique to recuperative, literary archeological projects, to "theoretically sophisticated" interventions, we might thus understand it to be a series of overlapping, discontinuous, and multiply interpretable discursive sites.

For example, Mary Helen Washington is perhaps best known for a series of anthologies that made black women's writing available to a wide readership. To call this work literary archaeology is to overlook the significance of her experiments with the conventions of anthologizing. In each of her collections, textual selections are interwoven with essays that are at once interpretive, contextual, and frequently autobiographical. Taken together, they perform the theoretical work of reconceiving influence, genre, the role of the editor, and the relationship of text to context.

▲ ▲ ▲ ▲ ▲

principally—but also sexuality and class—function as interrelated ideologies that can produce relations of domination and subordination but can also operate as sites of social change. Most importantly, they assume that there can be no black feminism without intersectionality. For as Cheryl I. Harris so aptly argues:

> Feminist discourse which fails to take account of race and anti-racist discourse that fails to take account of sexism disables and marginalizes the experience of women of color. Moreover, it leaves untouched critical dimensions of the structural apparatus of racial patriarchy—the particular system born in chattel slavery and carried to the present in the Contract with America. We thus remain vulnerable to the distorted images that are the dysfunctional products of prevailing racial and sexual ideologies.[19]

Black feminist reading, understood as reading intersectionally, thus directs our attention to the ways racism, misogyny, homophobia, and class discrimination have functioned historically and in the present to subordinate all black people and all women. By addressing the multifarious ways in which ideologies of race, gender, class, and sexuality reinforce one another, reading intersectionally can illuminate the diverse ways in which relations of domination and subordination are produced.

I do not intend this study to provide an exhaustive overview of the ways race and gender interact. Rather, this project both contributes to ongoing debates about the interdependency of various categories of experience and suggests other directions that studies of race, gender, and culture might take.

Split Affinities: Representing Interracial Rape

iven the history of profound, myriad connections between racism and sexual exploitation in the United States, interracial rape provides a productive site for considering the intersectionality of race and gender, second only to the institution of slavery. Myths of black male and female sexual appetitiveness were constructed to enable certain white men to exert their rights over the bodies of black men and white and black women during slavery, thereby inextricably linking ideologies of racial and gender oppression. The image of sexually inexhaustible black men was used to police relations between black men and white women and invoked in order to justify violence against black men. The myth of promiscuous slave women established a context within which white men could exercise their property rights upon the bodies of black women, and claim ownership of their offspring with impunity.

After slavery the slippage between racism and sexism assumed other forms; however, the specter of rape continued to victimize black men and women in related ways. Mobs of whites raped black women in order to restrict the progress of black communities as a whole and black men in particular.[1] In addition, especially during the period from Reconstruction through World War II, accusations of interracial rape were used to legitimate lynching, a form of random mob violence connected routinely to the alleged rape of a white woman by a black man, even when no evidence of sexual assault existed. Jacquelyn Dowd Hall has argued that the perceived connection between lynching and rape grows out of the construction of white women as "the forbidden fruit, the untouchable property, the ultimate symbol of white male power." This association in turn sets in motion a cultural narrative in which the rape of a frail white victim by a savage black male must be avenged by the putative chivalry of her white male protectors.[2]

In this chapter I consider some of the paradoxes and silences that emerge from the discourse of interracial rape. Drawing my examples from journalistic accounts, a short story by Alice Walker entitled "Advancing Luna—and Ida B. Wells," and my own experience of teaching that story, I examine some of the contradictions that arise within representations and debates around the rape of a white woman by a black man. I argue that these conflicts emerge at the mention of either an actual or an alleged interracial rape of this kind because of the way that narratives of the rape of a white woman by a black man have been used throughout U.S. history to perpetuate and sustain both racist and sexist oppression.

▲ ▲ ▲ ▲ ▲

Beginning with the highly publicized Tawana Brawley and Central Park Jogger cases, a series of high-profile cases involving sexuality and violence have galvanized popular and academic attention.[3] George Bush tapped into pervasive racial fears and sealed his bid for the presidency in 1987 when his television ad campaign associated Michael Dukakis's prison-leave program with the rape of a white woman by furloughed prisoner Willie Horton, a black man. By analyzing the nature of the language used in various contexts to discuss interracial rape, I explore how such incidents continue to inform and reflect the distribution of power in this country as well as our national identity, rooted as they are in the history of slavery, urbanization, and the law.[4]

The explosive coverage of actual or alleged cases of interracial rape (the Tawana Brawley case, the Central Park rape, the Willie Horton case, the Stuart murder case, to name but a few) and the political uses to which these cases have been put, suggest the myriad ways in which the history of slavery and lynching informs the construction of racial and gender relations in contemporary United States culture. I discuss the Central Park Jogger case in order to show how ideologies of racial and gender difference come into tension with and interrogate each other. I analyze the limits of the inflammatory rhetoric used by the mainstream, "white" press on the one hand and the "black" press on the other. I then examine the nature of black feminist responses to suggest the terms of a perspective informed by intersectionality. I discuss the narrative strategies of Walker's "Advancing Luna" because they display from another perspective a black feminist response to interracial rape. The chapter ends with a brief examination of some of the pedagogical issues that arose for me during my attempts to teach "Advancing Luna." In each context, I suggest that silences speak volumes, indicating the ways in which cultural anxieties about racial and gender difference are projected upon each other.

I

In her autobiography, *Crusade for Justice*, turn-of-the-century journalist and political activist Ida B. Wells argues that "[Lynching] really was...an excuse to get rid of Negroes who were acquiring wealth and property and thus 'keep the nigger down.'"[5] Wells's analysis acknowledges how the structure of gender relations and domination has been used to propel and facilitate racial oppression. Yet her opposition to lynching as a practice requires her effectively to deny the veracity of any white woman's testimony against a black man. Elsewhere in *Crusade* Wells discredits the testimony of an alleged rape victim even more directly. The classic situation she cites represents white women as willing participants in sexual relations with the black male victims of lynching. In one instance she argues that while white men assume the right to rape black women or consort with them, black men are killed for participating in any kind of sexual activity with white women: "these same white men lynched, burned, and tortured Negro men for doing the same thing with white women; even when the white women were willing victims." (71) The final clause, specifying the category of white women as "willing victims," takes precedence over the implied "unwilling victims" to whom Wells alludes earlier in the sentence. The following sentence elaborates upon the logic of the previous one, effectively blaming white women for the lynching of black men: "It seemed horrible to me that death in its most terrible form should be meted out to the Negro who was weak enough to take chances when accepting the invitations of these white women." (71) Wells's focus on the unreliability of white rape victims may well have been strategic, if not accurate, given the structure of race relations from the mid-nineteenth until the mid-twentieth centuries; as an antecedent, however, it presents difficulties for feminist critiques of interracial rape in the late twentieth century.

Wells's formulations subordinate the sexual to the racial dimension of interracial rape, thereby dramatizing the fact that the crime can never be read solely as an offense against women's bodies. It is always represented and understood within the context of a variety of issues surrounding race, imperialism, and the law.[6] As the media coverage and public response to recent criminal cases involving the hint, the allegation, or the fact of interracial rape demonstrate, a variety of cultural narratives that historically have linked sexual violence with racial oppression continue to determine the nature of public response to them.

For example, instances of interracial rape constitute sites of struggle between black and white men that allow privileged white men to exercise their property rights over the bodies of white women. As Angela Davis has shown, in the United States and other capitalist countries, rape laws, as a rule, were framed originally for the protection of men of the upper classes whose daughters and wives might be assaulted. By this light, the bodies of women seem decidedly less significant than the interests of their male superordinates.

In an article entitled "Rape, Racism, and the Law," Jennifer Wriggins argues that the differential sentencing of white and black convicted rapists exemplifies the way that rape law has been used to police the behavior of black men rather than to protect the rights of women to control their bodies and sexuality. During slavery, she writes:

> Statutes in many jurisdictions provided the death penalty
> or castration for rape when the convicted man was Black
> or mulatto and the victim white...The rape of Black
> women by white or Black men, on the other hand, was

legal...In those states where it was illegal for white men to rape white women, statutes provided less severe penalties for the convicted white rapist than for the convicted Black one.[7]

This kind of disparate treatment continues even into the present. Not only is the rape of a black woman by either a black or a white man treated less seriously by the criminal justice system and the media than the rape of a white woman, but black convicted rapists of white women are punished more severely than are white convicted rapists of white women. As Wriggins writes:

> Between 1930 and 1967, thirty-six percent of the Black men who were convicted of raping a white woman were executed. In stark contrast, only two percent of all defendants convicted of rape involving other racial combinations were executed. As a result of such disparate treatment, eighty-nine percent of the men executed for rape in this country were Black. While execution rates for all crimes were much higher for Black men than for white men, the differential was most dramatic when the crime was the rape of a white woman. (106)

These kinds of statistics suggest that the death penalty for rape was declared unconstitutional in 1977 at least in part because it enabled a kind of legalized lynching. Thus, in the aftermath of the rape and assault of the Central Park jogger, when Donald Trump and others directly or indirectly called for a return to the death penalty for convicted rapists, they were also, in effect, calling for a return to lynch law.

The rise of feminism from the late sixties through the present has done much to construct woman-centered anti-rape positions, although these responses sometimes reveal a racist bias. In the 1970s and 1980s rape emerged as a feminist issue as control over one's body and sexuality became a major area for concern

▲ ▲ ▲ ▲ ▲

and activism. Women addressed the need to break the silence about a pervasive aspect of female experience and to claim a space for themselves within the public discourse of race. From that beginning derived analyses of the place and function of rape within patriarchal culture. Moreover, feminists began to develop strategies for changing the legal and medical treatment of rape victims and the prosecution of perpetrators.

Susan Brownmiller's early study of rape, *Against Our Will: Men, Women, and Rape*, contributes prominently to analyses of the historical and cultural function of rape. Yet often it risks resuscitating the myth of the black rapist. Brownmiller, for example, argues that the history of the oppression of black men places legitimate expressions of male supremacy beyond their reach. They therefore resort to open sexual violence. In the context of her study, the wolf whistle that led to Emmett Till's lynching is read as a deliberate insult just short of physical assault.[8]

More recent feminist analyses improve upon Brownmiller's work by increasingly focusing on the interplay of issues of race and class within the context of gender relations. Susan Estrich, Angela Davis, and Catherine MacKinnon examine the implications of the fact that rape is the most underreported of all crimes and that the majority of rapes committed are intraracial.[9] Each shows in her respective argument how cultural assumptions about rapes and rapists protect privileged white men and continue to fetishize black male perpetrators. As MacKinnon writes:

> For every reported rape there are between two and ten unreported rapes; it is extremely important to ask not only why the ones that are reported are, but why the ones that are not reported are not.
>
> I think women report rapes when we feel we will be believed. The rapes that have been reported, as they have been reported, are the kinds of rapes women think will be believed when we report them. They have two qualities;

they are by a stranger, and they are by a Black man. These
two elements give you the white male archetype of rape.
When the newspaper says that these rapes are unusual,
they are right in a way. They are right because rapes by
strangers are the least common rapes women experience.
And to the extent that these are interracial, they are also
the least common rapes women experience. Most rapes
are by a man of the woman's race and by a man she
knows: her husband, her boss, an acquaintance, or a date.[10]

Given their position within the racial and gender hierarchy in
U.S. culture, it is not surprising that black Americans respond in
a variety of ways to instances of interracial rape. Within a context in which rape charges were often used to justify lynching or
legal execution, black men and women often perceive an accusation of rape as a way to terrorize innocent black men. This
kind of reasoning may lead to the denial of the fact that some
black men do rape. Alton Maddox, for instance, one of Tawana
Brawley's attorneys, leaped immediately to the defense of the
young men accused in the 1989 Central Park rape case and
demanded proof that a rape had actually occurred.

Black women's positions in relation to cases of interracial rape
are particularly vexed. As members of two communities under
siege, they may well sympathize with black males who stand
accused even as they share the victim's sense of violation. Yet that
identification with white women is uneasy, since black women
represent the most vulnerable and least visible victims of rape.
Their relative invisibility is to some degree rooted in the systematic sexual abuse to which they were subjected during slavery and
upon which racial patriarchy depends. The same ideology that
protected white male property rights by constructing black males
as rapists, constructed black women as sexually voracious. If
black women are understood always to be available and willing,
then the rape of a black woman becomes a contradiction in terms.

▲ ▲ ▲ ▲ ▲

The relative invisibility of black women victims of rape also reflects the differential value of women's bodies in capitalist societies. To the extent that rape is constructed as a crime against the property of privileged white men, crimes against the bodies of less valuable women—women of color, working-class women and lesbians, for example—mean less or mean differently than do those against heterosexual white women from the middle and upper classes.[11]

Given the nature of their history as rape victims, one might expect that black women would find common cause with white women in the anti-rape movement. Yet their own invisibility as victims within the movement, and a perceived indifference within the movement to the uses to which the fraudulent rape charge has been put, frequently have qualified their support.

The reporting of and response to a variety of recent cases involving the hint, the allegation, or the fact of interracial rape demonstrate the persistent and competing claims of these various cultural narratives upon the public imagination. I want here to comment briefly on the representation of the Stuart murder case and the Central Park rape, but certainly much remains to be said about many other cases, including the construction of the Tawana Brawley incident, and the uses to which Willie Horton was put in the Bush-Quayle campaign of 1987.

The Stuart murder case merits consideration in the context of a discussion about race and rape precisely because no allegation of rape was made. Despite the nonsexual nature of the alleged crime, the fiction of a black male perpetrator automatically sexualized a nonsexual crime, thereby displaying the profound and unarticulated links between race and sexuality.

Initially ascribed to a black gunman in a jogging suit, the October 29, 1989 murder of Carol Stuart in Boston was subsequently attributed to her husband, Charles, who committed suicide on January 4, 1990. The persistence and brutality of the

Boston police, who terrorized working-class black communities in search of a suspect, recalls the vigilante justice of earlier decades. The specter of interracial rape hovers over this case even though no specific allegations were made, witness the sexualized ways in which at least certain black men were interrogated. As Andrew Kopkind writes, "Young black men were stopped, searched and detrousered on the street for no cause more reasonable than their skin color. The cops called the blacks 'pussy' and 'faggot,' and sexual humiliation—white male power against black male impotence—became another disgusting tactic of the occupation."[12] We must take note here of the sexism and homophobia inherent in the policemen's tactics to investigate a crime against a woman. In the name of the body of a woman, the white policemen sought to humiliate black men by effeminizing them. Clearly, in this case the existence and identity of the victim became secondary to the power struggle between men.

The narrative linking sexual violence to racism is evident perhaps even more powerfully in the rhetoric surrounding the incident that has come to be known as the Central Park rape case. To review the details: on the night of Wednesday, April 19, 1989, a young white woman jogger was raped repeatedly and severely beaten in Central Park in Manhattan, allegedly by a group of black and Puerto Rican adolescent males between the ages of 14 and 17. In the hour before they attacked the jogger, the young men were reported to have been involved in at least four other assaults: they are alleged to have robbed a 52-year-old man; thrown rocks at a taxicab; chased a man and a woman on a tandem bicycle; and attacked a 40-year-old male jogger, hitting him on the head with a lead pipe. The rape victim, a highly-educated, 28-year-old investment banker who worked at Salomon Brothers, emerged from a coma after two weeks; besides the untold psychological damage, she also sustained irreversible neurological trauma.[13]

▲ ▲ ▲ ▲ ▲

The inflammatory rhetoric of the journalistic accounts of the Central Park rape reveals the context within which the narrative was constructed. In and of itself the crime was certainly heinous. Yet the media coverage intensified and polarized responses in New York City and around the country, for it made the story of sexual victimization inseparable from the rhetoric of racism.

From the tabloids—the *New York Daily News* and the *New York Post*—to the putatively more respectable *New York Newsday* and the *New York Times*, the mainstream press circulated and resuscitated myths of the bestial black rapist. In terms that recalled lynch law at the turn of the century, (then candidate, now Mayor) Rudolph Giuliani ran prime-time television advertisements calling for the death penalty for rapists, cop-killers, and serial murderers. Two weeks after the rape and assault, Donald Trump ran $85,000 worth of ads in *The New York Times, The Daily News, The New York Post,* and *New York Newsday* that called for the reinstatement of the death penalty and referred to the alleged assailants in the Central Park Jogger case. In his advertisement, Trump laments the passing of a period in the lives of New Yorkers when the police had the power to protect and help innocent people. "What has happened," he asks, "to the respect for authority, the fear of retribution by the courts, society and the police for those who break the law, who wantonly trespass on the rights of others?" "What has happened," he answers, is "the complete breakdown of life as we knew it."

According to Trump, New York families of all races have lost the freedom to stroll in the park, visit the playground, ride bicycles at dawn, or sit on their stoops because "roving bands of wild criminals roam our neighborhoods, dispensing their own vicious brand of twisted hatred on whomever they encounter." To those who would urge calm and moderation, embodied for Trump's purposes in former Mayor Edward Koch, Trump replies:

▲ ▲ ▲ ▲ ▲

I want to hate these muggers and murderers. They should be forced to suffer and, when they kill, they should be executed for their crimes. They must serve as examples so that others will think long and hard before committing a crime or an act of violence. Yes, Mayor Koch, I want to hate these murderers and I always will. I am not looking to psychoanalyze or understand them, I am looking to punish them. If the punishment is strong, the attacks on innocent people will stop. I recently watched a newscast trying to explain the "anger in these young men." I no longer want to understand their anger. I want them to understand our anger. I want them to be afraid.

I quote Trump's ad at some length for a number of reasons. First, although his language is more restrained than is some of the rhetoric I cite below, he does describe the accused as if they are subhuman or bestial, an association that recalls the conventional discourse of racism all too easily. Moreover, the language of the advertisement blurs the distinction between murderer and rapist, so that Trump effectively calls for the death penalty for muggers and rapists without explicitly doing so. And finally, the advertisement everywhere announces the presumption of the young men's guilt, an issue which becomes increasingly problematic in the weeks and months ahead.

News and feature stories were even more incendiary. On Friday, April 20, *The Daily News* headline announced: "Female jogger near death after savage attack by roving gang." The major story in that day's *Daily News* begins in the following manner: "A 28-year-old investment banker who regularly jogged in Central Park was repeatedly raped, viciously beaten and left for dead by a wolfpack of more than a dozen young teenagers who attacked her at the end of an escalating crime spree." The editorial in *The Daily News* that day begins:

▲ ▲ ▲ ▲ ▲

There was a full moon Wednesday night. A suitable backdrop for the howling of wolves. A vicious pack ran ram-
pant through Central Park. They attacked at least five people. One is now fighting for her life. Perhaps by the time
you read this, she will have lost that fight...This was not
shoplifting licorice sticks and bubble gum from a candy
counter. This was bestial brutality. "Mischief" is not mug-
ging. It is not gang rape. It is not beating someone's face to
a pulp with fists and crushing someone's skull with a rock.

This imagery of the young males as subhuman is then reca-
pitulated in articles and editorials in *The News* and the other New
York dailies. Indeed, in even the ostensibly more sedate *New York
Times*, an editorial dated April 26 is entitled "The Jogger and the
Wolf Pack." The editorial itself is replete again with imagery of
savagery and barbarity. Although the tone of the coverage is at
one level appropriate for the severity of the crime, the press
shaped the discourse around the event in ways that inflamed pervasive fears about the inhumanity of black men, offended comm-
munities of people of color, and perhaps most significantly,
pre-judged the accused. Further, the conventional journalistic
practice of protecting the privacy of rape victims by concealing
their identity, coupled with this victim's inability to speak, contributed to her further objectification. As a result, the young
woman became a pawn in the struggle of privileged white men to
regain control of their city.[14]

The mainstream media thus appropriated the discourse by
means of which the Central Park rape was decried; rather than
addressing the systemic violence and misogyny that makes
women unsafe in this society, the media articulated its critique in
terms that replicated racist stereotypes. In response to this kind
of inflammatory rhetoric, the black press went to the other
extreme, in many instances leaping to the defense of the young
men, whom they constructed as victims of a racist law enforce-

ment and judiciary system, virtually ignoring the existence of the woman they allegedly raped and beat.

Coverage of the crime in *The New York Amsterdam News* and *The City Sun,* both New York weekly black papers, always condemned the rape and assault; however, in article after article, the journalists subordinated the crime itself to other issues. For instance, in the weeks immediately following the Central Park rape and assault, *The Amsterdam News* carried front page stories about the rapes of black women in Brooklyn and Manhattan and about the trial of a white Harlem pastor accused of fondling, raping, and sodomizing black women in his congregation. These stories certainly served to publicize the victimization of black women by white and black men alike; nevertheless, they were showcased in order to undermine either tacitly or explicitly the visibility of the Central Park case. To use but one example, on the front page of the May 6, 1989 edition of *The Amsterdam News*, under a headline that reads: "Another Woman Raped and Strangled to Death: Police have no suspects, motive for brutal killing," the lead article by Harold L. Jamison begins: "A little over a week after the Wall Street banker, [was] allegedly raped and beaten by a group of teens, Manhattan police began without fanfare and hoopla, an investigation into the strangulation death of an African-American woman found raped and murdered in Fort Tryon Park."[15] In this instance, the Central Park Jogger case is invoked as part of the frame of an article about the rape and murder of a woman of color. The ironic reference to the police and the press, and the ambiguous placement of the adverb "allegedly" detract as well from the seriousness of the victim's condition.

In addition, the two papers early on challenged the way the young men were represented in other media, questioned the culpability of the accused and sought to direct attention away from the alleged perpetrators and toward political and socio-economic factors. An editorial on the front page of the April 29, 1989 edition of *The Amsterdam News*, written by editor-in-chief Wilbert A. Tatum and entitled "[Mayor Edward] Koch must resign" focuses on the victimization of the alleged perpetrators and downplays the severity of the crime against the victim. In Tatum's prose, references to the woman's condition are relegated to dependent clauses that subordinate the assault to the black community's wrath:

> As a young and talented white woman who is yet nameless lies near death in Metropolitan Hospital after an alleged assault and rape by eight African-American kids, an entire city is up in arms, as much in fear of their own lives, as in a mood for retribution. As much as we mourn for this [woman] and pray to whatever Gods may be for her complete recovery, we are angered too. We are angered by a mayor whose first reaction to this New York tragedy was to characterize the youngsters as "monsters," and defy anyone who would suggest that there could be a societal reason for such a crime. To be sure, it was an incomprehensible act; but by branding those who are not yet tried or convicted of a crime as "monsters," or anything else for that matter, only serves to further polarize a city that the mayor has already done an incredible job of polarizing.[16]

On page three of the same issue, journalist Jamison writes an extended article about the attack that subordinates the condemnation of the crime to black people's skepticism about the way the crime has been represented and constructed in the media and in the city as a whole. Black elected officials such as Congressman Charles Rangel of Manhattan and then-Manhattan Borough President David Dinkins censure the crime unproblematically. Other community "leaders" cited, whose voices dominate the article, contextualize the crime rather than discussing it directly. Rev. Calvin Butts of the Abyssinian Baptist Church attributes the violence displayed in this incident to the systemic problems that led to the murder of Michael Stewart at the hands of transit police in Brooklyn and that of Michael Griffith in Howard Beach. Father Lawrence Lucas of the Resurrection Roman Catholic Church in Harlem warns African Americans not to show so much outrage over the crime that they "make fools of themselves." He says "'On the same day of the attack, at 12:10 in the afternoon, in broad daylight, on 145th and Adam Clayton Powell Blvd., thugs using semi-automatic pistols killed one innocent bystander and injured two others; and we hardly [heard] a [whimper] from the media.'"[17]

In the same article, community activist Elombe Brath compares the situation of these young men to that of the Scottsboro Boys, nine black men wrongfully accused of raping two white women in 1931. This comparison is picked up and elaborated by Peter Noel in the May 3–9, 1989 issue of *The City Sun* in an article entitled "Rape and Class: From Scottsboro to Central Park."[18] In his article, Noel interweaves the Central Park narrative with the Scottsboro story in order to underscore the similarities between the two cases. However, Noel's comparison requires him to downplay the central difference between the two cases — in the Central Park case, a rape and assault definitely occurred, whereas in the Scottsboro case the women were apparently neither raped nor otherwise injured. His analysis of the similarities between the two cases requires him to focus on the perpetrators and de-emphasize the crime, thereby eliding the body of the victim.

The black press also chose to name the victim, thus violating the code observed by the mainstream press, to guard the privacy of rape victims. The way in which her name was used in the black press is particularly troublesome. *The Amsterdam News* justifies this decision by comparing its violation of the jogger's privacy with the mainstream media's publishing of the names of the juvenile alleged perpetrators, thereby equating the status of the victim with that of the alleged assailants. Moreover, *The*

▲ ▲ ▲ ▲ ▲

Amsterdam News points to the inconsistency of the media's policy of identification; since the mainstream press reveals many other details about the jogger (including her alma mater, employer, and photograph) it might as well publish her name. *The Amsterdam* critiques this kind of evasion as merely duplicitous; it would seem to me that this strategy of identifying the victim by her accomplishments and acquisitions contributes to a climate in which the privileged status of the victim determines the nature of public response to her circumstances. My sense again is that the black press works out its anger at the racism of the media and the larger society at the expense of the jogger.

In the immediate aftermath of the rape and assault, the coverage in the black press appeared profoundly misogynist and blindly defensive. However, during the trial, it became evident that the prosecution had virtually no forensic evidence linking the accused to the crime. The first three young men to go to trial were sentenced on the basis of their confessions, all of which seem to have been acquired in an irregular, if not illegal manner. Defense attorneys for Yusef Salaam and Antron McCray, two of the defendants in the first trial, have argued that as juveniles they should not have been Mirandized outside the presence of their parents. During the trial, Detective Thomas W. McKenna admitted to tricking Yusef Salaam into confessing his role in the rape and beating. And Kharey Wise, who was in the second group of young men to be indicted, was questioned for twenty-four hours beginning at midnight on the evening of the attack before he confessed.[19] Thus the rhetoric of the black press and self-styled black spokesmen such as Alton Maddox, while clearly misogynist, may not have been as irresponsible as it first appeared.

Nevertheless, if the mainstream media racialized the language by which the crime was censured, the black press denied the seriousness of the crime in order to critique the ways in which the young men were represented and handled in the press and in the judiciary system. The limits of each position reveals the need for a discourse that can condemn the violence and misogyny of the crime, and censure the crime as well as the criminal, without either falling back on racist language or pre-judging those who might well be innocent. What is needed is a discourse attuned to the racism that surrounds the case, the misogyny that enabled it, and the connections between the two. What is needed is a critique that acknowledges the competing claims of race and gender.[20]

In a special section of the May 9, 1989 *Village Voice*, a series of articles by four black writers, Cathy Campbell, Linda Goode Bryant, Greg Tate, and Lisa Kennedy, suggest the contours and functions of responses that address the interlocking mechanisms of race and gender and complicate the polarized positions articulated within the major media, black and white. Each writer breaks up familiar connections, such as those between racism and rape or victimization and innocence. The essays are marked as well by a collage effect by means of which the writers articulate the various subject positions they occupy and bring to bear upon the issue.

In "The Victim Trap: Don't Believe the Hype," Cathy Campbell responds to the danger in what she sees as the defense attorneys' tendency to associate viciousness with oppression. As she writes: "Since when was viciousness a simple index of oppression? Committing such a vicious crime doesn't mean that these deviants are more representative victims of white racism than the rest of us; furthermore, the overwhelming majority of us are struggling to overcome this victimization—not condone gang-rape in our name." (31)

In lieu of the predictable comparison between Central Park and Howard Beach, comparisons that rely on the elision of sexual violence, Campbell invokes the Tawana Brawley case. But rather than asking why the apparent rape and assault of a black woman is prosecuted differently than are those of a white woman, Campbell examines the nature of the sexual violence and misogyny revealed in that case as well. (Campbell believes, as I do, that even if Brawley made up her story in order to escape her stepfather's wrath, she is still the victim of sexual violence.) Campbell's argument shows that a discourse that addresses both a particular crime and the context within which it occurs need not be motivated by an attempt to minimize the perpetrators' culpability.

The collage effect to which I alluded earlier appears subtly in each essay, but operates visually and most vividly in Linda Goode Bryant's article, "Running on Empty: A Mother's Fears." Bryant intersperses a narrative of her own private fears with her analysis of the attack. The italicized portions of the essay recount her fears for her own, her daughter's, her son's, and her brother's varying vulnerability to random attack and harassment within a misogynist and racist culture. In the non-italicized sections of the essay she analyzes her reaction in the wake of the Central Park rape case. Hers is a position that at once identifies with the victim, links the crime to misogyny within black and white communities, identifies with the mothers of the accused, and decries the racism of her employers. The patchwork quality of the narrative is an apt figure for the complex, often conflicting reactions the crime invokes.

The title of Lisa Kennedy's essay, "Body Double: The Anatomy of a Crime," refers to the way in which the press both diminishes the significance of the crime as an assault against the body of a woman even as it constructs the body of a monolithic black community. Kennedy names and explores the space black feminist rage ought to occupy in this discourse, rendering explicit, as does Bryant, the profound links among polemical, analytical and personal discourse:

As a black woman, I find myself in a schizo state of

mind, my body fragmented beyond thought: woman or black? Is it possible to resist the to-and-fro of that identity, and try to speak from my body? These are the times that try my black woman's mind, when every word is measured for what it will cost my body. If I accept the premise of the coverage, that this rape is more heartbreaking than all the rapes that happen to women of color, then what happens to the value of my body? What happens to the quality of my blackness? (36)

My critique of the representation of the Central Park case in the media and the differential application of rape laws is not tantamount to an argument for less rigorous policies of reporting and punishing rape. Rather, I argue here implicitly for more consistent investigative procedures, and more consistent sentencing—whoever the victim and whoever the perpetrator may be. Moreover, I advocate a woman-centered rape law policy that seeks to police violent, coercive sexual behavior as a crime in and of itself, one that recognizes that rape is part of a system of aggression against all women that includes domestic violence, incest, and sexual harassment.[21]

Most explicitly, I advocate here as well an increased awareness of the problematic role of the media in contemporary culture. I address the representation of the Central Park case as largely discursive, but with "real-life" consequences. Even as someone trained and pre-disposed to critique media representations, I realize retrospectively that when I first began to work on this case, I believed in the young men's guilt even as I criticized the coverage of the event, because the mainstream media so frequently juxtaposed descriptions of the crime with descriptions and images of the accused. Over time, however, it has become increasingly clear that while someone surely assaulted the jogger, it is not at all certain that the young men arrested, indicted, and sentenced were the perpetrators. In which case, it does seem

▲ ▲ ▲ ▲ ▲

that the media, in collusion with the police department and the prosecution, destroyed any possibility for a fair trial. The role of the press must be aggressively critiqued in such instances, not only from within, in the guise of the by now obligatory self-analyzing story in which a staff writer comments upon the role of the media. Rather, the discursive strategies of the press must be critiqued from outside, from the perspectives of those who are able to see "both/and."

II

Unacknowledged cultural narratives such as those which link racial and gender oppression structure our lives as social subjects; the ability of some to maintain dominance over others depends upon these narratives remaining pervasive but unarticulated. In my teaching, both in courses that are explicitly about black feminism and those that are not, I take seriously the responsibility to teach texts by and about black women, and to develop strategies for discussing the ways in which interactions between race and gender are inscribed in narrative. However, it is equally important to me to work with my students toward the recognition of the kinds of silences that structure the social hierarchy in which we live.

The teaching of texts about "border cases" such as interracial rape, makes more explicit for students the theoretical principles of "intersectionality" that inform my courses. A story such as "Advancing Luna—and Ida B. Wells," by Alice Walker, prompts students to speak from a variety of perspectives on the issue of interracial rape.[22] To the extent that the story foregrounds the range of positions that different women assume around the subject, it requires readers to acknowledge as well the extent to which we keep secret our responses to such cases. My goal in teaching a work such as this one is to enable students to develop a vocabulary for addressing the differences between them that necessarily exist.

I return to this particular story because of the way it confronts the issue of difference. I teach it additionally because it is representative of Walker's less well-known, but to me more interesting fiction. *The Color Purple*, which continues to be one of the more frequently taught works written by Walker, raises knotty questions about sexual violence, and the construction of race and sexuality. Yet for me, the utopian vision with which the novel ends disappoints and undermines the complexity of narration and characterization that has gone before. In contrast, "Advancing Luna" and the other stories included in Walker's 1981 collection entitled *You Can't Keep a Good Woman Down*, individually and collectively confront the inadequacy of representation and eschew easy resolutions. This story calls attention to the unspeakability of interracial rape; others in the volume address issues having to do with the representation of, for example, the female body, or the relationship between racial and gender politics.[23]

Moreover, a discussion of "Advancing Luna" seems to me to be especially pertinent in a feminist classroom because it self-consciously participates in a variety of discourses, thereby problematizing the boundaries between literature and theory, literature and "real life." By thematizing one of the central paradoxes of the black feminist enterprise, it is simultaneously narrative and theory. It exemplifies the tendency that Barbara Christian identifies for writers of color "to theorize in narrative forms, in stories, riddles and proverbs, and in the play with language."[24] Moreover, to the extent that the narrator function breaks down and is replaced by an author figure or function who establishes a relation with narratives of the lives of "real people," the story presents itself as simultaneously fiction and fact/autobiography.

In the first two paragraphs of the story, the unnamed narrator/protagonist, a young black woman, establishes significant differences between herself and Luna, a young white woman with

▲ ▲ ▲ ▲ ▲

whom she worked in the movement and with whom she subsequently shared an apartment in New York. As the story develops, the space between them becomes increasingly resonant, charged with anger, betrayal and the specter of sexual competitiveness.

"Advancing Luna" opens in the summer of 1965 in Atlanta at a political conference and rally. Within the context of the Civil Rights movement, the narrator is endowed with the advantages of both race and class—in this case her status as a black woman and a student. The narrator/protagonist is thus an insider among the high-spirited black people graced with a "sense of almost divine purpose."[25] An undergraduate at Sarah Lawrence College, she feels doubly at home in this "summery, student-studded" revolution (85). Luna is no doubt also a student, but the narrator represents her as an outsider, passive, and wan. While the narrator characterizes herself as bold and energetic, Luna tentatively awaits the graciousness of a Negro home. To emphasize the space between them, the narrator confidently strides through Atlanta instead of riding in the pickup truck with Luna.

The narrator's hostility toward Luna is nowhere more evident than in her description of her. Here she inscribes her hostility on Luna's body in the process of anatomizing it. Moving from her breasts to the shape of her face to her acne to her asthmatic breathing, she renders Luna a configuration of inadequacies. Moreover, the idiosyncratic organization of the paragraphs of description makes it that much harder to conceive of Luna as a social or narrative subject:

> What first struck me about Luna when we later lived together was that she did not own a bra. This was curious to me, I suppose, because she also did not need one. Her chest was practically flat, her breasts like those of a child. Her face was round, and she suffered from acne. She carried with her always a tube of that "skin-colored"

(if one's skin is pink or eggshell) medication designed to
dry up pimples. At the oddest times—waiting for a light
to change, listening to voter registration instructions,
talking about her father's new girlfriend, she would
apply the stuff, holding in her other hand a small brass
mirror the size of her thumb, which she also carried for
just this purpose. (86-87)

The narrator's hostility to Luna is evident not only in the way
in which she anatomizes her, but also in less direct ways. For
instance, by suggesting that Luna's skin is "skin-colored" she
blames her for conforming to the image of the ideal Clearasil user.
By means of the disruptive logic of the passage, the narrator cari-
catures her. She interrupts the order of a physical or spatial description to catch Luna, as if unawares, in the midst of the uncompli-
mentary, repeated activity of applying her acne medication.

In the next paragraph, the narrator's hostility toward Luna takes
the form of momentarily erasing her from her own description:

We were assigned to work together in a small, rigidly seg-
regated South Georgia town that the city fathers, incon-
gruously and years ago, had named Freehold. Luna was
slightly asthmatic and when overheated or nervous she
breathed through her mouth. She wore her shoulderlength
black hair with bangs to her eyebrows and the rest brushed
behind her ears. Her eyes were brown and rather small.
She was attractive, but just barely and with effort. Had she
been the slightest bit overweight, for instance, she would
have gone completely unnoticed, and would have faded
into the background where, even in a revolution, fat people seemed destined to go. (87)

Although Luna is not fat, the narrator says she is the sort of
person who would have faded into the background if she were.

During the summer of 1965, Luna and the narrator become

friends through their shared work. The story focuses primarily on their life together in New York where they share an apartment the following year.

The first exchange between the narrator and Luna that is actually dramatized in the text is one in which Luna admits to having been raped by a black man named Freddie Pye during her summer in the South. This conversation explains the source of the narrator's retrospective hostility to her. The narrator resents Luna for having spoken of the rape; her characterization is a way of punishing her for the admission. In addition, the description might be read as an attempt to undermine Luna's testimony by denying her desirability. By sexually denigrating Luna, the narrator indirectly blames her for her own victimization. This hostility points to a thinly-veiled sexual competitiveness between the black and the white woman which may more generally problematize the discourse of interracial rape.

Immediately after Luna's revelation, the story begins to break down. The narrator is unable to position herself in relation to Luna's testimony; as a result, the trajectory of the narrative disintegrates. The narrator's first reaction is to step out of the present of the text to historicize and censure the rape—she reads it in the context of Eldridge Cleaver's and Imamu Amiri Baraka's defenses of rape. Responding to Luna's position as a silenced victim, the narrator asks why she didn't scream and says she felt that she would have screamed.

As the exchange continues, almost involuntarily the narrator links the rape to the lynching of Emmett Till and other black men. Then, instead of identifying with the silenced woman victim, she locates herself in relation to the silenced black male victim of lynching: "I had seen photographs of white folks standing in a circle roasting something that had talked to them in their own language before they tore out its tongue."(92–93) Forced to confront the implications of her split affinities, she who would have screamed her head off is now herself silenced. First embarrassed, then angry, she thinks, but does not say, "'How dare she tell me this!'"(93)

At this point, the narrative shifts to one of its first metatextual moments. Here it is no longer focused on the narrator/protagonist's and Luna's conversation about the rape, but rather on the narrator/author's difficulty in thinking or writing about interracial rape. The narrator steps out of the story to speculate and theorize about the exclusion of black women from the discourse surrounding rape. The conversation at this juncture is not between Luna and the narrator, but between the narrator and Ida B. Wells—or rather, with an imaginary reconstruction of Wells's analysis of the relationship between rape and lynching.

The issue of rape thus forces a series of separations. Not only does it separate the narrator from Luna, but it also separates the narrator/protagonist from the narrator/author. Moreover, Luna's admission generates a series of silences. In an oddly and doubly counter-feminist move that recalls Wells's own discrediting of the testimony of white victims, the narrator wants to believe that Luna made up the rape; only Luna's failure to report the crime— her silence—convinces her that the white woman has spoken the truth. Indeed, in the final section of the main portion of the story, silences function as a refrain. Luna "never told [the narrator] what irked her" (97) the day the narrator had two white male friends spend the night at their apartment, even though that event marked the ending of their relationship. The two women never discussed the rape again; they "never discussed Freddie Pye or Luna's remaining feelings about what had happened."(97) Perhaps most strikingly, they never mention Freddie Pye's subsequent visit to the apartment during which he spends the night in Luna's bedroom. It is as if the subject of interracial rape contains within itself so many unspeakable issues that it makes communication between the black and the white woman impossible.

▲ ▲ ▲ ▲ ▲

Near the end of the main portion of the story, the narrator mentions Freddie Pye's return visit without explicit comment. By failing to explain the relation of his visit to Luna's story, the narrator suggests that Luna's word is unreliable. Luna's position is further undermined by the anecdote with which this section ends. This portion concludes with the story of Luna's visit to the narrator's home in the South several years later. On this occasion Luna brings a piece of pottery which is later broken by the narrator's daughter. The narrator remarks that in gluing the pot back together she "improves the beauty and fragility of the design." (98) This claim yet again bestows authority upon the narrator over and above Luna's power.

What follows are four other "endings" to the story. The narrator's inability to settle on one underscores the unnarratability of the story of interracial rape. Further, each ending absents the narrator from the story, absolving her of responsibility for the account and raising issues about the possibility of representation. It is as if the conflict between her racial and her gender identity has deconstructed the function of the narrator.

The first in this series of metatextual sections, entitled "Afterwords, Afterwards Second Thoughts" emphasizes again the unresolvability of the account. Told from the perspective of a voice that suggests that of the author, it discusses her inability to conclude the story.[26] On the one hand, she would have liked to have used a conclusion, appropriate for a text produced in a just society, in which Luna and Freddie Pye would have been forced to work toward a mutual understanding of the rape. Given the contradictions around race and gender in contemporary culture, however, she is left with an open ending followed by a series of sections that problematize even that one.

The second appended section, entitled "Luna: Ida B. Wells—Discarded Notes" continues this exploration of the relationship between narrative choices and ideological context. This section acknowledges the nature of the selections that the narrator/author has made in constructing the character of Luna. In "Imaginary Knowledge," the third appended section, the narrator creates a hypothetical meeting between Luna and Freddie Pye. This ending is the one that the author figure of the "Afterwords" section says would be appropriate for a story such as this were it published "in a country truly committed to justice." (98) In this cultural context, however, she can only employ such an ending by calling attention to its fictionality: she says that two people have become "'characters.'" (101) This section is called "Imaginary," but the narrator will only imagine so much. She brings Luna and Freddie to the moment when they would talk about rape and then says that they must remove that stumbling block themselves.

The story ends with a section called "Postscript: Havana, Cuba, November 1976" in which the author figure speaks with a muralist/photographer from the United States about "Luna." The muralist offers a nationalist reading that supplants the narrator's racial and gender analysis. In this section it becomes clear that the attention has shifted away from the narrator and the significance of her interpretation, to Freddie Pye and his motivations. The lack of closure in the story, as well as the process by which the narrator recedes from the text, all suggest that the story is unwriting itself even as it is being written.

III

I once taught "Advancing Luna" in a seminar on Black Women Writers in the United States which was evenly divided between black and white women undergraduates. In this seminar students would occasionally argue about interpretations or dispute the ascendancy of racial or gender issues in the texts under discussion, but we seemed for the most part to arrive at consentaneous readings of the texts we discussed. This particular experience of teaching "Advancing Luna" dramatized within the classroom the very divisions that operate at the level of narrative within the story itself. I found it to be a story that breaks various codes of silence even as its own narration breaks down.

The tendency toward unanimity that characterized this seminar may well have been a function of our collective response to the syllabus and to the composition of the class. A teacher of African-American literature in integrated classrooms at elite, predominantly white universities, I tend to foreground the accessibility of the texts to all students even as I articulate the strategies and components that reveal their cultural specificity. I further suspect that the students and I at some unexamined level assumed that our disagreements notwithstanding, as a community of women we would be able to contain differences within some provisional model of consensus. "Advancing Luna" forced us to confront the nature of differences that could not be resolved and to acknowledge the difficulty of speaking across them.

This story silenced a group of ordinarily talkative students in a number of ways. When I asked them where they positioned themselves in the story, no one would answer. My students then began to deconstruct the question, asking what it meant to "position" or "locate" oneself in a narrative. As our discussion progressed, they began to admit that, in fact, they did know where they positioned themselves. They were embarrassed or frightened by their positionalities, however, and could not speak through that self-consciousness. For example, several white students finally admitted that they located themselves with Luna. I prompted them to discuss her motivations, and was struck by the extent to which students who are otherwise careful readers had manufactured an entire inner life for Luna. It was as if they were compensating unintentionally for silences in the narrator's representation of her character.

▲ ▲ ▲ ▲ ▲

During the course of the conversation, it became clear that the black women students who spoke sided with Freddie Pye, the white women who spoke, with Luna.[27] Once this split became evident, then my project became to get the students to articulate their differences. My hope was that the black students would claim their divergent affinities with the black man on racial grounds and the white woman on the basis of gender, and that the students would recognize the cost of their respective identifications. For it was important to me that they acknowledge the implications of their discomfort, the extent to which they felt betrayed by their divisions from each other.

To my mind, within the space of a classroom students should be able to develop a vocabulary for speaking across differences that are initially the source of silences. Perhaps more importantly, I would hope that they would begin to develop a sense of respect for each other as the individual products of discrete cultural and historical experiences. Not surprisingly, however, I cannot claim that in my seminar I was able to achieve either of these goals. No doubt we only managed to enact the fraught and fragile nature of the issues that divide us. The story forced the students to confront the circumstances of their own embodiment. It perhaps also required them to confront my embodiment. The story might thus be seen as a "border case" in and of itself, for it illuminated the silences upon which our consensus depended.

The process of teaching (and then writing about the teaching of) this story required me to confront the limits of what a class and a syllabus can accomplish. Not only were we unable to reach any kind of satisfactory closure in our discussion on "Advancing Luna," but moreover, our discussions of subsequent texts did not seem to take place at a heightened level of consciousness. I can therefore only allow myself the guarded hope that in this instance, as is so often the case in teaching, a few students will comprehend the impact of our experience of this text at some point in the future.

Faced with the conundra of classroom and text, the only closure available to me (as is the case with Walker's author figure) is the metatextual. I would argue that what Walker and her narrator confront in writing "Advancing Luna" and what my students confront in discussing the story is the status of the text as a specific cultural formation that reflects and shapes their experience as social subjects. The issue of an incident of interracial rape (for our purposes here, one involving a black man and a white woman) sets in motion a variety of historical, cultural, and ideological narratives and associations. Mutually contradictory, and rooted deeply in cultural practice, these embedded narratives and associations impinge upon our attempt to articulate positions around an instance of interracial rape.

IV

I once overheard someone say that all of the talk about race and class in relation to the Central Park rape was beside the point.[28] For this person, it was a crime about gender relations: in Central Park on April 19, a group of young men raped a young woman. Race and class had nothing to do with it.

To the extent that the crime seems not to have been racially motivated, this person's reading of the incident seems to be true at one level. Yet at another level, the comment seems strikingly naive, for neither the perpetrators nor the victim are purely gendered beings. To paraphrase Teresa de Lauretis, men and women are not purely sexual or merely racial, economic, or (sub) cultural, but all of these together and in conflict with another.[29]

From a sociological point of view, columnist Tom Wicker wrote in the April 28 issue of the *New York Times* that the crime was racial because the attackers lived surrounded by the social pathologies of the inner city and that these influences have had consequences on their attitudes and behavior. He also argued that the crime was racial to the extent that it exacerbated racial tensions in the metropolitan New York area.

To his observation, I would add that to the extent that the discourses of race and rape are deeply connected, cases of interracial rape are constituted simultaneously as crimes of race and of gender. To acknowledge that cultural narratives are inescapable is to recognize that cases such as this one always engage and participate in ideologies of gender, race, and class. Rather than attempting to determine the primacy of race or class or gender, we must search for a deeper understanding of how these categories of experience inflect and interrogate each other and constitute us as social subjects.

Class and Gender
in Narratives
of Passing

Stories of racial passing have long captivated the attention of
American viewers and readers.[1] These accounts of characters
who are "legally" black yet light-skinned enough to live as
white have fascinated the American imagination for a variety of
reasons. I suspect that they compel, at least in part, because they
force the reader to confront a range of conflicts that are raised
but inadequately explored in the classic texts within the genre.
In this chapter I consider some of these paradoxes as sites that
reveal the interconnections among race, class, and gender in the
U.S. context. I locate passing within the discourse of intersec-

tionality because although it is generally motivated by class considerations (people pass primarily in order to partake of the wider opportunities available to those in power), and constructed in racial terms (people describe the passing person as wanting to be white, not wanting to be rich), its consequences are distributed differentially on the basis of gender (women in narrative are more likely to be punished for passing than are men).[2]

I begin by showing how the hierarchization of race and gender in John Stahl's *Imitation of Life* (1934) reinscribes certain conventions of the genre and manipulates spectatorial allegiances. I argue that a reading informed by the theory of intersectionality resists such a narrative and emotional logic.[3] In the second section, I discuss two more recent works that problematize the assumptions of the passing plot: Julie Dash's *Illusions* (1982) and Charles Lane's *True Identity* (1991). These newer texts presuppose to some degree the intersectionality of race and gender, and thereby construct passing as a potentially subversive activity.

The narrative trajectories of classic passing texts are typically predetermined; they so fully naturalize certain givens that they mask a range of contradictions inherent within them. For instance, they presuppose that characters who pass for white are betrayers of the black race, and they depend, almost inevitably, upon the association of blackness with self-denial and suffering, and of whiteness with selfishness and material comfort. The combination of these points—passing as betrayal, blackness as self-denial, whiteness as comfort—has the effect of advocating black accommodationism, since the texts repeatedly punish at least this particular form of upward mobility. These texts thus become sites where anti-racist and white supremacist ideologies converge, encouraging their black readers to stay in their places.

Jessie Redmon Fauset's 1928 novel *Plum Bun*, for example, associates the aspirations of her protagonist, Angela Murray, with crass materialism and contempt for her race. As a child, Angela often passes with her mother, Mattie, when they are out on the town for the day, although the narrator makes clear that Mattie passes only for convenience and self-indulgence; she has no desire to be white. Here the narrative betrays one of its central tensions. However innocent Mattie's intentions may appear to be, they have dire consequences. She and her husband are both killed off indirectly in the text because of her passing. Moreover, it leads Angela to decide to live her life as a white woman, a decision for which she atones throughout much of the novel.

Given her racial, class, and gender status, Angela can only gain access to white privilege through the agency and good will of a wealthy white man, in this case, a man named Roger Fielding. Fielding does not know that she is black, but he does know that she is poorer than he; as a result, he refuses to marry her and offers only to set her up as his mistress. After Roger ends their relationship and dashes Angela's hopes, she recognizes the limitations of her desires; eventually she reveals her racial identity and is allowed to share her life with the black man she loves.

In the Murray family, racial politics and narrative approbation follow loosely the distribution of pigmentation. While Angela develops an appreciation for material comforts from her light-complexioned mother, her darker father and sister (Junius and Virginia) are more concerned with using their talents to uplift the race. Angela is constructed as merely self-indulgent; Virginia is virtuous, diligent, and bold. A fiercely committed race woman, she tells a friend who considers moving to South America in order to avoid racism in the United States that:

> We've all of us got to make up our minds to the sacrifice of something. I mean something more than just the ordinary sacrifices in life, not so much for the sake of the next generation as for the sake of some principle, for the sake of some immaterial quality like pride or intense self-respect or even a saving complacency; a spiritual

tonic which the race needs perhaps just as much as the body might need iron or whatever it does need to give the proper kind of resistance. There are some things which an individual might want, but which he'd just have to give up forever for the sake of the more important whole.[4]

Angela's materialistic goals jeopardize her financial stability; Virginia possesses greater security because she uses her talents productively and lives within her means. Her virtues notwithstanding, Virginia endures the humiliation of a sister who is unable to acknowledge her publicly. However, once Angela accepts her race, she and Virginia are reconciled and Virginia is reunited with her true love.

Given the legal basis of the notion of passing, it is not surprising that classic passing narratives seem ideologically self-contradictory. Narratives of passing, whether written by African-American or by white authors, presume the African-American internalization of the "one-drop" and the related "hypo-descent" rules. According to the one-drop rule, individuals are classified as black if they possess one black ancestor; the "hypo-descent" rule, acknowledged historically by the federal courts, the U.S. census bureau, and other agencies of the state, assigned people of mixed racial origin to the status of the subordinated racial group. Originally deployed as a means of supporting the slavocracy and the Jim Crow system of racial segregation, then, these "rules" were internalized by African Americans who converted them from mere signifiers of shame to markers of pride.

The accommodationist impulse that seems to unify the racist and anti-racist agendas is frequently enabled through the figure of the black mother. The limited opportunities that "home" represents are often associated with the self-sacrificing maternal body, where conservative racial and gender ideologies are typically lodged in narrative. The sentimental weight this figure bears

▲ ▲ ▲ ▲ ▲

in works such as the novel and two film versions of *Imitation of Life* (the other being Douglas Sirk's 1959 remake), Oscar Micheaux's *God's Stepchildren* (1938), and Elia Kazan's *Pinky* (1949) obstructs a resistant spectatorial gaze. Because these works all conflate the light-skinned daughters' rejection of their own subordinate status with their rejection of their mothers, readers or viewers are manipulated into criticizing rather than endorsing these non-compliant light-skinned women.

Additionally, while the logic of these texts for the most part condemns passing as a strategy for resisting racism, in fact, several actually use this racialized politic specifically to restrain the options and behavior of black women. Passing male characters can either be re-educated and returned to the bosom of home and community to uplift the race, or they can remain in the white world and be constructed with some measure of condescension, ambivalence, or even approval.[5] Passing women characters, on the other hand, are either re-educated and returned to the bosom of home and community, or they receive some extreme form of punishment such as death or the sacrifice of a loved one.[6]

A more general paradox or conflict exists in the very syntax of the formulation "legally black yet physically white," for the phrase polarizes the two terms and invokes ostensibly stable categories of racial difference. Systems of racial oppression depend upon the notion that one can distinguish between the empowered and disempowered populations. Those boundaries that demarcate racial difference are best policed by monitoring the congress between members of opposite sexes of different races. Yet the bodies of mixed-race characters defy the binarisms upon which constructions of racial identity depend. Signs of the inescapable fact of miscegenation, they testify to the illicit or exploitative sexual relations between black women and white men or to the historically unspeakable relations between white women and black men. The light-skinned black body thus both invokes and transgresses the boundaries between the races and the sexes that structure the American social hierarchy. It indicates a contradiction between appearance and "essential" racial identity within a system of racial distinctions based upon differences presumed to be visible.

Black Female Spectatorship and *Imitation of Life* (1934)

Based on Fannie Hurst's bestselling novel of the same name, John Stahl's *Imitation of Life* enjoyed extraordinary popularity in its day. Yet its reliance upon stereotypic depictions of the black mother as mammy provoked widespread criticism on the part of its contemporaneous black and other anti-racist viewers and of early critics of black images in Hollywood film. More recently, it has attracted the attention of feminist film critics and theorists because of the way it situates race within the context of the maternal melodrama.[7]

While there may appear to be a veritable industry of *Imitation of Life* criticism, most focuses on Douglas Sirk's 1959 remake. Judith Butler's 1990 essay centers on this version as does Lucy Fischer's 1991 volume, *Imitation of Life*, which contains essays, reviews, and the continuity script. Indeed, among recent studies of the *Imitation of Life* phenomenon, only Sandy Flitterman-Lewis's "*Imitation(s) of Life:* The Black Woman's Double Determination as Troubling 'Other,'" and Lauren Berlant's "National Brands/National Body: *Imitation of Life*," pay equal attention to the two films.[8]

Sirk's film has attracted more notice partly because of its comparative stylistic sophistication. As Fischer has written, the film "was released during the decline of the classical cinema and the birth of the modernist movement...*Imitation*, with its exaggerated generic codes, embraced the art film's ironic stance toward transparent style." (4) Indeed, critics have commented on the extent to which, in Sirk's remake, imitation becomes the dominant thematic; the self-reflexive quality of this film in particular but of his other work as well exposes the artifice of the medium as well as the decay and disintegration of the social relations that organize contemporary culture.[9] Moreover, the film's preoccupation with issues of artificiality makes it especially suitable for arguments that explore the cultural construction and contestation of gender and race.

The comparative sophistication of the 1959 *Imitation* notwithstanding, I find the 1934 version better suited to my purposes here. The cynical Sirk remake narrativizes its status as spectacle, allowing viewers and critics to keep it at arm's length, bracket their emotional responses, and read its strategies primarily as comments on the constructedness of ideologies of race, gender, sexuality, and performance.[10] In contrast, the relative "sincerity" of the Stahl film implicates viewers more directly in the effects of specific constructions of race and gender relations; a critique of the project of this film thus brings sharply into focus the work of the resistant spectator in the passing narrative.

My interest in the film derives from the relationship between the main or white plot, dominated by the top-billed white star, Claudette Colbert, as Bea Pullman, and the subordinate or black plot, which features Louise Beavers as Delilah, the black mother, and Fredi Washington as her daughter, Peola. Like the book upon which it is based and the 1959 remake, this version of *Imitation of Life* is fundamentally concerned with the problematic of the white working mother and advocates the return of white women to their domestic spaces and relations. However, these issues are raised much more explicitly both in the novel and in the 1959 remake. In the 1934 version the anxiety about Bea's career and choices remains largely absent from the plot within which she figures centrally. Here the mother-daughter relationship in the main plot is idealized, if not made comedic. Tensions surrounding motherhood, class mobility, and abandonment are displaced onto the black plot, which performs the emotional labor in the film much as Delilah in Bea's household performs the visible domestic labor. Bea, the absent, largely ephemeral white mother is reconstituted in Delilah, the hyperembodied, present black mother. Moreover, the anger reserved for women who leave their place in this film is directed at Peola, who wants more for herself than the opportunities that segregationist U.S. culture will allow her. Gender and racial ideology are thus profoundly connected; Peola's character bears the weight not only of her abandonment of Delilah, but also of Bea's "abandonment" of Jessie.

And yet, while these displacements and the content of the plots may presuppose the interdependence of the lives of the two women and their daughters, the strategies by which meaning is conveyed—structure, tonal shifts, soundtrack, and camera work—differentiate and hierarchize the two plots. This stylistic disarticulation constructs gender as tenor, race as vehicle, so that the problematics of race in the film are deployed as mere metaphors for gender relations.

I argue here that the film conflates differences within and between black and white women through the relation between the two plots. I suggest, moreover, that a resistant, black feminist reading disaggregates the film's construction of the nexus of race and gender and refuses the dominance of the putative main plot in order to expose the various ways black women's bodies are used to teach whites on both sides of the camera a lesson. This reading is consistent with Toni Morrison's discussion of the functions that Africanist characters have served in U.S. cultural discourse, for it shows how the black characters are used as "surrogates and enablers," in order to "limn out and enforce the invention and implications of whiteness," and to allow the white subject to meditate upon his or her own humanity.[11] One need only look at the uses to which African Americans are typically put in much Hollywood and independent cinema today to realize that these constructions persist.

Imitation of Life is the rags-to-riches story of Bea Pullman, a white widow, and mother of a daughter named Jessie. In the opening sequence, Bea, the Colbert character, is crumbling under the conflicting demands of mothering and working in the maple syrup sales business. As the film begins, she struggles to bathe and dress Jessie and fix breakfast when she receives a call from an important customer. While she speaks on the phone, the coffee boils over, the oatmeal begins to burn, and her daughter calls out for her. The intimate opening scene thus soon gives way to a frenzy of activity; Bea races up and down a flight of stairs, juggling several responsibilities and performing none of them well. She is clearly not in her place and doesn't even seem to know what that place is.

At the precise moment when Bea seems most overwhelmed, the massive, nurturant, tireless Delilah Johnson, played by Louise Beavers, appears at her door, offering to come live with her and take care of her and her daughter in exchange for nothing more than food and shelter for herself and her fair-skinned daughter, Peola. In contrast to Bea's frenetic quality, Delilah enters the film circumscribed in her place. The shot-reverse-shot editing of the scene of their meeting underscores this observation. When Delilah rings the bell, Bea runs down the stairs to answer it. The camera focuses on Bea's face as she looks toward the doorway and then a tracking shot follows her across the kitchen to the door. The next shot quickly zooms in on Delilah's beaming face framed by the screen door against a softly lit pastoral background. The effect here is to momentarily freeze Delilah's face in a nostalgic, photographic stillness.

The camera here suggests more than simply the women's mutual acknowledgment. Rather, the matching of the tracking shot with the close-up, zoom, reverse shot contrasts the two women's positions, thereby establishing the disparate functions each serves in the film. While Bea is associated with economic mobility and progress, Delilah is immediately constructed as a figure of stability, and of timeless, mythic qualities. And of course, the myth she conjures up is that of the mammy in the plantation South. Unable to negotiate her way through the urban setting—her inability to distinguish Astor Street from Astor Avenue is what leads her to Bea's home in the first place—she is eager to assume the position of an unpaid laborer. Once Delilah joins Bea's household and assumes primary responsibility for her home and child, Bea's life becomes immediately more organized and manageable. The parallel households become one, with the two women forming, to borrow Lauren Berlant's term, "a quasi-companionate couple."[12]

But Delilah gives Bea more than domestic assistance. She shares with her the recipe for her irresistible pancakes, a product that Bea markets so successfully that in time it makes her a millionaire. As her fortunes improve, Bea "generously" bestows upon Delilah twenty percent of the Aunt Delilah Corporation, and promises her that she'll be rich. Bea offers Delilah her own house and car, and the following exchange takes place:

> *Delilah*: You gonna send me away, Miss Bea? I can't live wid ya? Oh, honey chile, please don' send me away—don' do that to me.
> *Bea*: Don't you want your own house?
> *D.*: No'm. How'm I gonna take care of you and Miss Jessie if I ain' here? Let me an' Peola stay same's we been doin'. I's you' cook an' I want to stay you' cook.
> *B.*: Well, of course you can stay, Delilah. I only thought, now that the money's coming in,—and, after all, Delilah,

it's all from your pancake flour.
D.: I gives it to you honey. I makes you a present of it.
You'se welcome.

This scene is immediately followed by a shot of boxes of pancake flour, emblazoned with a picture of Delilah's beaming face, topped with a crisp chef's hat, sliding down the rollway of a packing machine and then swirling into a bin filled with thousands of these boxes. This shot then fades into one of a large neon sign that advertises the product. First it reads "Aunt Delilah's Pancake Flour: 32,000,000 Packages sold last year." Then it flashes an image of Delilah flipping pancakes.

The juxtaposition of these two scenes is significant for a variety of reasons. The content of the conversation between Bea and Delilah recalls the static quality of Delilah's initial appearance in the film. A domestic servant in the 1930s, she is the apologists' vision of the plantation mammy revisited, devoid of any desire other than to care for her white mistress, even after emancipation. As such, she offers the perfect justification for black repression. The symbolic power of this image is underscored by the ensuing shots in which we see how fully the type has captivated the popular imagination. The repeated image of the face on the box not only signals the passage of time and marks metaphorically Bea's accomplishments. The proliferation of the image shows as well the vast marketability of the mammy as type.

Bea's business accomplishments are accompanied by personal gratification. The few glimpses we see of her interactions with her daughter indicate that the two women take great delight in each other. Moreover, at one of her gala parties, she meets ichthyologist Stephen Archer, with whom she falls passionately in love. Indeed, the romance that ensues is presented as having reawakened her sexuality and womanhood; realizing where her priorities ought to lie, she stays away from the office for weeks on end, basking in Stephen's affections.

But while Bea's life proceeds from one fulfilling experience to the next, Delilah's sufferings proliferate, due to her tortured relationship with Peola. However easily Delilah may accept her role, Peola refuses to do so. Each time the movie attempts to soar into an idyllic fantasy about Bea's charmed personal or professional future, Peola is there to return it to earth with her relentless demands for equality and acceptance.

This sort of segregation of plot function is evident even as the opening credits roll. The first piece of music we hear might be identified as Delilah's theme: the opening phrase of "Nobody knows the trouble I seen," sung by a choir. The phrase is then repeated in an orchestral arrangement, heavy with strings, up an interval of a third. The soundtrack then segues into what I call Bea's theme, a light, bouncy melody dominated by harp and arpeggios. The phrase from the spiritual conjures up a certain sadness; the refusal to complete the line (with "Nobody knows but Jesus") leaves the singer and the listener in a state of desiring. In contrast, Bea's theme demonstrates greater musical range and is allowed to reach its completion. The tension between pleasure and pain on which the narrative depends is thus anticipated by the juxtaposition of the musical themes.

In the narrative, scenes of pleasure featuring Bea and Jessie frequently alternate with those of Delilah's and Peola's suffering. For instance, after Bea has paid off all the debts she incurred in order to open her first business, she and Delilah fantasize about how they will spend their money when they become rich. Bea dreams of taking a vacation, but Delilah only wants to be able to get off her feet. The placidity of the scene in which the two women share their secret hopes is disrupted when Peola enters, crying "I'm not black! I'm not black! I won't be black! Jessie called me that!" Despite Bea's reproaches, Delilah insists that Peola must learn to accept her place, saying, "You gotta learn to take it and you might as well begin now." When Bea asks Jessie how she could say "such a mean, cruel thing to Peola," Delilah responds," It ain't her fault, Miss Bea. It ain't your'n and it ain't mine. I don't know rightly where the blame lies. It can't be our Lord's. It's got me puzzled." This is the first of a number of episodes in which Peola expresses her anger at her situation in the form of anger at her mother. She cries, "You! You! It's 'cause you're black! You make me black!" Of course, her accusations allude to the laws governing slavery, by which the child "followed the condition" of the mother.

The camera work in this scene contributes to the way we respond to the various characters' situations. Bea and Jessie are shot in medium two-shots, either facing each other or standing side-by-side watching Delilah console Peola. This choice distances viewers from them and, in turn, distances them from the intensity of Delilah's and Peola's interaction and Delilah's suffering, even though Jessie precipitated it. In contrast, the medium two-shots of Delilah and Peola emphasize the discord between the two: while Delilah cradles her to her capacious bosom, Peola insults her. The close-ups of Delilah register her pain at and acceptance of her daughter's verbal abuse and encourage viewers to identify with her suffering rather than with Peola's rebelliousness.

This dynamic between a sequence that celebrates Bea's achievements only to culminate in Peola's anger and violence is replicated throughout the film. It's as if Peola and Delilah are repeatedly scapegoated. Their circumstances provide the source of viewer tears. Moreover, their respective frustrations and hurts pay for Bea's yearnings to rise above her place. For instance, in the next scene when Jessie is home sick from school on a stormy day, we see Bea caring for her at her bedside in an idyllic moment of maternal nurturance. Meanwhile, Delilah goes to the school to take Peola her scarf and coat. When she arrives and asks for Peola, she learns that the child has been passing. Furious at having been found out, Peola says to her mother once outside the classroom door, "I hate you ...I hate you."

After Bea's business has made her and Delilah wealthy and they move into a townhouse in Manhattan, Bea throws an elaborate party at which she meets the man who becomes her fiancé. Delilah vicariously enjoys the party from their downstairs apartment, but Peola's position below the stairs causes her to suffer. Here Bea's social success is intercut with the tense scenes between Delilah and Peola; Peola repeatedly refuses the comfort and company Delilah offers her. The sequence ends in a teary scene between the two women in which Peola agrees to attend a "Negro" school in the south. Delilah's stoic acceptance of her daughter's contempt and her articulation of Christian resignation make explicit the religious subtext of her characterization and enhance the sentimental appeal of her character.

The scene in which Jessie comes home from her boarding school for vacation and meets Stephen Archer for the first time promises to be another idealized moment. That encounter, too, ends abruptly when Delilah rushes in with the news that Peola has disappeared from the colored teachers' college she attends. Delilah and Bea leave immediately to find Peola, and discover her working as a cashier in a coffee shop near the school. Once again, Delilah unmasks Peola publicly. This time, after they return home, Peola announces her intention to pass, to deny her blackness and her mother. After a long, tearful scene, Delilah agrees to let her daughter go, and dies soon thereafter. A contrite, distraught Peola returns home in time for the funeral, and hurls herself upon the coffin, but the only reconciliation possible is symbolic.

In contrast, just after Delilah swears to renounce her daughter, Bea meets Jessie on the stairs and affirms the unassailability

CLASS AND GENDER IN NARRATIVES

of their relationship. The movie threatens to rupture Bea and Jessie's vow. While Bea and Delilah are off looking for Peola, Jessie is falling in love with Stephen, her mother's lover. Clearly, like Peola, Jessie no doubt wishes as well to do away with her mother. But since Delilah in fact does die, there is no real need for Bea to do so. Instead, when Bea learns of this conflict, she resolves that nothing and no one can come between her and her daughter, so she breaks her engagement to Stephen. In the final shot of the film, Bea and Jessie embrace while Bea repeats the lines that Jessie speaks at the beginning of the film: "I want my quack quack. I want my quack quack." Sandy Flitterman-Lewis glosses this ending usefully when she writes:

> [Bea's] nostalgic tone indicates a yearning for that untroubled unity, the simplicity of mother-daughter sharing which she has attempted to recapture through her sacrifice of romance. This circularity signifies a reassertion of the utopian maternal which in fact structures the entire film; the atavistic reference to an originary moment of dual reciprocity implies an isolation from all social context, from all difference and disturbance.[13]

Although the film constructs a symmetrical household with two single mothers and two daughters, in fact the emotional logic sets up an analogy between the white mother and the black daughter. As the novel and the 1959 film demonstrate, the situations of these two women invite comparison more easily than do those of either the two mothers or the two daughters: these are the two women who leave their rightful place; these are the two who must be returned to those places at the end of the film.

The film denies the legitimacy of both Bea's claim for a public life and Peola's for social equality. But it requires Peola's punishment to stand in for Bea's; this also explains why her desires for independence and equality are constructed as inseparable from her rejection of her mother's love. Her desire is shown to be analogous to what is seen as Bea's neglect of her daughter, Jessie, and her punishment is designed to teach both her and Bea a lesson.

In order to establish Peola's story as a metaphor for Bea's, the film glosses over the radical differences between the two women's circumstances. It's one thing for Bea to stay in her place (by the end she is a millionaire), another altogether for Peola to stay where she belongs as the daughter of a black domestic worker. Put another way, this structuring device depends simultaneously upon the spectacularization of difference—in this case, racial difference—and the denial of the meanings that historically have attached to those differences.

To the extent that the film attempts to disaggregate class and race from gender identity, a resistant, black feminist analysis of this film would refuse such a denial of the implications of class and racial difference for gender identity. This is not to say that such ideological commitments would protect an oppositional viewer from the sentimental effects that the film produces; however, redefining these connections would disrupt, at least partially, the overdetermined logic of the film.

Clearly, a resistant spectator would question the premise of the film that either Bea or Peola should remain in her place. Likewise, such a spectator would challenge the inevitability of the film's logic, that the desire for racial equality is tantamount to a desire to betray either the race or the mother. An intersectional critique emphasizes as well the extent to which race and gender are linked in both plots, witness the incommensurate distribution of consequences. Both Bea and Peola refuse to remain in the positions to which they have been relegated. But race and class privilege provide a safety net below which Bea cannot fall. Peola's class advantages ultimately cannot protect her from the power of race and gender inequities.

▲ ▲ ▲ ▲ ▲

Contemporary Revisions of the Passing Plot

During the party at which Bea meets Stephen, Delilah and Bea meet in the hallway of the mansion in which they live. Delilah descends the stairs to her quarters and Bea goes back up to the party. Indeed, throughout the party Peola and Delilah remain in their downstairs apartment; the situation is rendered all the more problematic by the fact that Delilah is dressed in a flowing gown, as if to enjoy Bea's party vicariously. The staircase here, leading up and leading down, bifurcates the screen into Bea's realm and Delilah's. It is a visual reminder of the construction of stable racial identities and differences upon which this classic passing narrative depends.

In contrast, recent texts that center on the passing plot eschew the sorts of rigid divisions that inform their antecedents. Julie Dash's *Illusions* and Charles Lane's *True Identity* seek to emancipate passing as a phenomenon from its overdetermined plots, deploying it instead to unmask the interconnections of racial and gender ideologies. By invoking and subverting traditional uses of the narrative, the films inscribe the position of spectatorial resistance.

Illusions

Julie Dash's *Illusions* centers on Mignon Dupree, a black woman studio executive in 1940s Hollywood who uses her ability to pass in order to try to bring stories to the screen that will reveal the untold histories of people of color. Unlike her narrative antecedents, for whom passing is constructed as an all-or-nothing, reactionary proposition, Mignon passes discontinuously; the film suggests that she is motivated to pass by a desire to serve her race. For not only does she have a black lover and remain in close contact with her family, but she works to get fair wages for Esther Jeeter, a black singer hired to match her voice to the image of a lip-synching white star. At the end of the film, Lt. Bedsford, the white male colleague who has been sexually harassing Mignon confronts her with his discovery of her secret; however, we are left not with Mignon's humiliation, but with her passionate vow to stay in Hollywood and continue fighting.

Unlike other passing characters, whose fates are frequently marked and sealed symbolically with signs of their fallen or marginal status, Mignon is associated with signs that connect her to African American cultural history and practice.[14] When we first see her, the camera focuses on the v-shaped black and white pattern in her suit and the black veil that partially conceals her face. As Phyllis Rauch Klotman reminds us, during World War II, "for African Americans the double 'V' (official NAACP sign) meant victory over racism at home as well as victory abroad." Klotman notes further that the veil recalls DuBois's famous metaphor for the color line, a barrier Mignon transgresses more or less at will.[15] The multiplicity of meanings that attach to these symbols point to the nuances of her characterization. Her representation contrasts with a figure such as Naomi, the protagonist of Oscar Micheaux's *God's Stepchildren*, who appears on screen twice marked with an "x"—once over her head on her hat, and once on the straps of her evening dress across her back—as if to emphasize her inability to escape her fate as a woman marked by her presumptive mixed racial origins.

The anticlimatic nature of Bedsford's accusation and the iconography associated with Mignon both signal Dash's revisionist approach to her subject. Typically in passing texts, the precariousness of the character's decision provides the central tension of the narrative. Like the character, the reader or viewer is haunted by the imminence of exposure and punishment. In

▲ ▲ ▲ ▲ ▲

*Illusion*s, in contrast, passing is only one of a series of decep-
tions with which the film is concerned. Chief among these is the
constructedness of the medium itself.

As the film begins, Mignon quotes from Ralph Ellison's
Shadow and Act, thereby framing the film with a reminder that
cinema itself is only illusory:

> To direct an attack upon Hollywood would indeed be to
> confuse portrayal with action, the image with reality. In
> the beginning was not the shadow but the act, and the
> province of Hollywood is not action, but Illusion.

Her remarks are juxtaposed with Lt. Bedsford's press release
about the centrality of cinema to the war effort. For Bedsford, a
Signal Corps officer assigned to Hollywood to produce war
films, representations of the war are as significant as is the war
"itself"; he sees motion pictures as crucial to the work of the mil-
itary. Unlike Ellison *cum* Mignon, who warns against confusing
portrayal and action, he emphasizes their interdependence:

> As a grim and determined nation marshals its manpower
> and its vast material resources to meet the totalitarian
> challenge to the democratic way of life, the motion pic-
> ture industry is privileged to stand in the very forefront of
> the united American endeavor....The industry's broad
> sphere of service in the war effort is perhaps without par-
> allel. The fact that no other medium is so adapted to the
> task of building and sustaining national morale on both
> the fighting and home fronts, readily attests to the motion
> picture's essentiality.

The point of greatest narrative interest and tension is the scene
in the rerecording stage, for there the passing plot and the exploration of cinematic illusion are brought together. Mignon embodies in the extreme the way that black women in particular (and

▲ ▲ ▲ ▲ ▲

members of all disenfranchised groups in general) depend upon masquerade to protect themselves and exercise power. As if to emphasize this aspect of her character, she functions as a sort of ventriloquist throughout the film. We know about Julius, her lover, and her mother because they speak through her.[16] In this scene in the rerecording stage, where sound and image must be matched, Dash alludes to the significance of masquerade in the production of cinematic illusion as well as racial and gender identity.

In the first clip from the film on which the sound engineer and his assistant are working, white starlet Lila Grant sings and dances with two male performers. The synch here is fine, but this sequence signals the dilemma at the heart of the situation as it unfolds. Here, Lila lip synchs to a tune by Ella Fitzgerald.[17] The blond starlet's appeal is enhanced by the fact that she scoffs at the cello and songs "soft and mellow," preferring instead the power of the "rhythm man." Fitzgerald herself is of course disappeared from the frame altogether; her voice and the spontaneity to which the lyrics allude are marketable on film, but her body and bodies like it are at odds with the image of womanhood in which the medium traffics.[18]

The overdubbing of Lila's second song with Esther Jeeter's voice dramatizes the evacuation of black women's power and the mutually constitutive relations between both black and white womanhood and race and gender identity. Esther's talents and labor, both invisible within the finished product, maintain Lila's position on and off screen. To the extent that the film allows for black female subjectivity and experience, they circulate within the marketplace only when they can be packaged within a real or illusory white woman's body. Likewise, the identity of the idealized white female subject relies upon rendering invisible her dependency upon the labor and identities of black women.

Dash's dramatization of the race and gender politics of this use of overdubbing critiques white power and visibility.

However, it does not presuppose an essentialized, authentic black female subject. By choosing to have Esther herself lip synch over Fitzgerald's vocals, Dash concedes her own implication in the construction and production of black women's identity. Problematizing her own position, she reminds us that her film is no more "real" than the one on which Mignon works.

True Identity

Directed by Charles Lane, *True Identity* revises the passing plot to highlight the role of performance in and destabilize constructions of racial difference. *True Identity* centers on Miles Pope (played by Lenny Henry, a black British comic known for his impersonations). Miles is an aspiring actor in Manhattan who dreams of being cast as a dramatic lead and fantasizes about playing Othello. However, the limited availability of serious dramatic roles for blacks in theatre makes it hard for him to find suitable work. In an early scene, Miles first resists and then capitulates to his acting coach's insistence that he play a pimp "more black…more Afro-American…more Harlemesque." This scene questions the meaning of authentic blackness, an issue to which the film returns repeatedly. The coach attempts to prompt Miles to play the part of a "real" black person, but true blackness to him is entirely artificial, constructed out of the images that commonly circulate as black in popular representations of black culture. Miles's character in the film undermines this conception of black character; he seeks a way to perform black masculinity as something other than a crotch-grabbing pimp who lives in Harlem.

Miles's agent Harvey sends him to Florida for what Miles believes will be a starring role in a production of *A Raisin in the Sun*. But as it turns out, Miles has been cast as a California raisin in a breakfast cereal commercial. On his return flight, he discovers that he has been seated next to Leland Carver (Frank Langella), the owner of the theatre at which the current New York production of *Othello* is being staged. The plane comes close to crashing as it approaches Kennedy Airport; in the moments of panic that precede what appears to be almost certain death, Carver confesses to Miles that he is really Frank Luchino, a Mafia kingpin who is believed to have been killed in an explosion years before. Thanks to the wonders of plastic surgery, he has taken on a new life and established a new identity as Carver, a financier and arts philanthropist.

Miraculously, the plane does not crash. Carver and Miles both realize that Miles knows too much about Carver's past and that his life is now endangered. Indeed, Carver's assistant, Anthony, a hold-over from his days as a full-time mobster, tries to kill Miles before he can leave the airport.

Because the police and the FBI cannot protect him, Miles goes to his best friend, Dwayne, a makeup artist (played by director Lane), for help. Dwayne makes him up as a white man so that he can hide from Carver and his hit men; Dwayne encourages the reluctant Miles to think of this deception as "the performance for his life."

When Miles, in white face, returns to his apartment to pack his bags, he meets and accidentally kills Carver's hit man, La Motta. As he contemplates his next move, Carver's deputy, Anthony, breaks in, assumes that Miles in white face is La Motta and La Motta, whom he has never seen, is Miles's neighbor. Thus Miles's alternative identity is born. To maintain his disguise, he must feign not merely the gestures and inflections of a "white" man, but more specifically, he must imitate those associated with media representations of Italian-American gangsters.

The rest of the film is given over largely to Miles's attempts, as La Motta, to pretend to pursue himself, as Miles, while he really seeks evidence that will identify Carver as Luchino. He reveals his "true identity" to Carver's black female interior dec-orator, Kristi (Anne Marie Johnson), with whom he falls in love, and persuades her to help him search Carver's house. Meanwhile, Dwayne helps him stage his own murder, so that in the short run, Carver believes that Miles really is dead.

As a result of an elaborate sequence of events, Miles is cast as Othello in the production at Carver's theatre. When Carver discovers that Miles is still alive, he plots his assassination on stage during the opening night performance. But Miles, Dwayne, and the FBI successfully thwart his plan; Carver is unmasked and finally captured.

Like *Illusions, True Identity* dismantles several of the inevitabilities that have become associated historically with the passing plot. First, it breaks up the conventional associations of passing with the boundary between black and white to show that it is a phenomenon that may be deployed strategically within a specific racial group. Frank Luchino/Leland Carver does not simply assume the identity of a legitimate businessman. An Italian American by birth, he passes as a white Anglo-Saxon Protestant philanthropist complete with suburban mansion, sophisticated blond wife (Peggy Lipton), and restrained inflec-tions and polished diction. His bilinguality or biculturalism is revealed during his conversations with Anthony and "LaMotta." In these scenes his gestures become more emphatic, and his speech is characterized by the dropped final "g," as well as the intonations, the sharp dentals, and the profusion of expletives associated with ethnic New York (especially Italian-American) stereotypes. This use of Luchino/Carver has the potential to complicate monolithic constructions of whiteness. However, its satiric potential is undermined by the reliance upon Italian-American stereotypes in the constitution of Luchino's "true identity," especially within a film that critiques the conflation of black stereotypes with "real" black experience.

Second, like Mignon's, Miles's passing is discontinuous; it does not conform to the all-or-nothing model upon which the passing plot typically depends. Granted, Miles's options are rather more limited than are those of his fair-skinned antecedents, since his ability to pass is entirely artificial (he only looks white when he wears a wig and makeup). Nevertheless, he is shown to have more control over his alternatives than do passing characters in earlier texts, given that he can change racial identification more or less at will.

Third, Miles's decision to pass is not associated automatically with betrayal of the race. His decision to pass is motivated by the impulse to self-preservation. Yet he remains committed to a politics of racial solidarity, as evidenced in a sequence involving two taxicabs. Shortly after Miles assumes his identity as a white man, he watches a well-dressed black man try and fail to hail a taxicab on a New York street. Miles stands behind him and raises his hand; the next cabdriver stops immediately for Miles who yields the taxi to the darker man. This scene assures the viewer that Miles has not turned his back on the indignities to which African Americans are routinely subjected, even though he has become "white." Moreover, it gestures to "real world" racism within a context where racial identity is being performed.[19]

When the next taxi arrives, a white woman tries to claim that she saw it first. After a brief struggle both leap in and give the driver contradictory directions. As the taxi pulls off, the woman looks at Miles, "reads" him as white and middle class, and tries to figure out why he looks familiar. Eventually she decides that she must recognize him from the offices of Merrill Lynch. Rather than trading on white skin privilege to bond with a woman who he suspects would recoil from him under other circumstances, Miles slips into "black style" and tells her he has just gotten out of prison for robbing a bank in Queens. The terrified woman leaps from the taxi at the next opportunity.

▲▼▲▼▲

Although this scene is played for comic effect, it serves to mark the limits of Miles's commitment to his performance and it reminds us of the power of the cultural narratives of race and gender from which we can never fully escape.

The fact that the protagonist is an actor and his best friend a make-up artist highlights the significance of performance in the construction of racial identity in the film. The media may construct blackness according to certain types which, like all stereotypes, have some basis in the historical circumstances of real people. But these images are only part of the story. Miles's performance as pimp, Othello, Darryl Brown (James Brown's fictional brother), Frank La Motta, indeed, even Lenny Henry's performance as Miles Pope himself, points to a range of black (and indeed white) types and indicates the extent to which racial identity is shaped by issues of class, region, and nation.

Although Miles chooses political and racial solidarity over assimilation, the film seems to deconstruct a unifying, authentic notion of black identity. Yet even as *True Identity* challenges the binary opposition between black and white and the association of the black underclass with racial authenticity, it allows familiar correspondences between women's appearance and subjectivity to persist without interrogation. The diminutive Dwayne has a penchant for large black women, a predilection that allows the film to return repeatedly to visual and verbal images of over-sexed, corpulent, mouthy, dark-skinned women. The women to whom the film grants intelligence and tact—Kristi and Mrs. Carver (Peggy Lipton)—conform to more conventional standards of black and white women's beauty. Thus, *True Identity* employs the passing plot to explore the intersectionality of race and class, but it does not confront adequately the extent to which gender identities are constituted likewise by race and class.

◄ ◄ ◄ ◄ ◄

Conclusion

Passing narratives lend themselves to mutually contradictory interpretations. For some readers and critics, these texts are inherently conservative, for they reinscribe the dynamics of white skin privilege by focusing our readerly attention or spectatorial gaze on characters light enough to pass for white. For others, the presence and discussions of such characters are more broadly suggestive. As Hazel Carby has argued, for example, these characters may be read as markers of the space between white privilege and black disempowerment.[20]

I have tried to recuperate certain of these texts through a strategy of reading that resists equating the desire for equality (especially on the part of black women) with the desire to be white. I have been concerned with what it means to punish characters who pass. But I am finally convinced that passing narratives do not provide an unproblematic way out of the discourse of racial essentialism. Passing for white will answer neither the obstacles of misogyny nor those of racism. The conditions of passing narratives are, however, productive sites for considering how the intersectionality of race, class, and gender ideologies are constituted and denied; not only do bodies that pass function as markers of sexual and racial transgression, but they signal as well the inescapable class implications of crossing these boundaries.

Authenticity in Narratives of the Black Middle Class

For his 1993 anthology, *Lure and Loathing: Essays on Race, Identity, and the Ambivalence of Assimilation*, Gerald Early invited twenty black intellectuals to respond to the most famous passage from W. E. B. DuBois's *The Souls of Black Folk* (1903):

> After the Egyptian and Indian, the Greek and Roman, the Teuton and Mongolian, the Negro is a sort of seventh son, born with a veil, and gifted with second-sight in this American world—a world which yields him no true self-consciousness, but only lets him see himself through the revelation of the other world. It is a peculiar

sensation, this double-consciousness, this sense of always looking at one's self through the eyes of others, of measuring one's soul by the tape of a world that looks on in amused contempt and pity. One ever feels his twoness—an American, a Negro; two souls, two thoughts, two unreconciled strivings; two warring ideals in one dark body, whose dogged strength alone keeps it from being torn asunder.

The history of the American Negro is the history of this strife—this longing to attain self-conscious manhood, to merge his double self into a better and truer self.

Although Early rightly shows that the implications of this passage are myriad and complex, it is commonly cited to suggest the tension between hegemonic and resistant constructions of group or individual identities. The "other" to whom DuBois refers in this passage is typically understood to be whites; DuBois describes black subjects who experience themselves always through the mediating gaze of a white spectator.

Several of Early's contributors (among them Glenn C. Loury and Reginald McKnight) situate their experience of DuBoisian doubleness not at the color line, but at the class line. For them, the question of what it means to be black and middle class inflects the question of what it means to be black and American.[1]

The concern for what it means to be black when one also enjoys educational, economic, or cultural privilege has recurred in debates about race and identity throughout the twentieth century. Franz Boas, mentor and advisor to Zora Neale Hurston and Du-Bois, and one of the earliest anthropologists to study black folklore in the United States, believed that racial identity was located in indigenous cultural practices; to his mind, knowledge of such practices had the power to counteract prevalent notions that African heritage was a source of shame. He feared that the rise of public education encouraged black self-loathing and reinforced

▲ ▲ ▲ ▲ ▲

myths of white supremacy. His work on black folklore could thus be read as associating unadulterated racial identity with the black poor and uneducated and racial assimilation with the educated.

This belief in an authentic racial experience unmediated by exposure to "white" cultural influences recurs in subsequent discussions of black cultural identity, usually in opposition to hegemonic theories and practices that are perceived as denying the existence of African-American culture. For instance, E. Franklin Frazier constructed a model of the black bourgeoisie as a deeply troubled people, uprooted from black traditions and alienated from those of their white counterparts.[2] And Harold Cruse attributed what he perceived to be the dissolution of black "intellectual and artistic capital" to the assimilationist longings of the black middle class.[3]

Literary figures as well contributed to these discussions around the issue of racial authenticity. In "The Negro Artist and the Racial Mountain," a classic essay from the Harlem Renaissance published in *The Nation* in response to "The Negro-Art Hokum" written by conservative journalist George Schuyler, Langston Hughes, himself a product of the black middle class, associates racial purity with the working class and assimilation with economic privilege. He begins the essay with an anecdote about another young poet from the "Negro" middle class who "wants to be a poet—not a Negro poet." He imagines that the poet comes from a family that associates whiteness with all that is beautiful and admirable and concludes that "it would be [difficult] for an artist born in such a home to interest himself in interpreting the beauty of his own people."[4]

Hughes contrasts this vision of black middle class assimilationism with the "low-down" folks who he believes resist the coercive power of hegemonic culture. His version of working-class resistance both appreciates African-American culture and inspires black art:

> [The] low-down folks, the so-called common ele-
> ment...live on Seventh Street in Washington or State
> Street in Chicago and they do not particularly care
> whether they are like white folks or anybody else. Their
> joy runs, bang! into ecstasy. Their religion soars to a
> shout. Work maybe a little today, rest a little tomorrow.
> Play awhile. Sing awhile. O, let's dance! these common
> people are not afraid of spirituals, as for a long time their
> more intellectual brethren were, and jazz is their child.
> They furnish a wealth of colorful, distinctive material for
> any artist because they still hold their own individuality
> in the face of American standardizations. And perhaps
> these common people will give to the world its truly
> great Negro artist, the one who is not afraid to be him-
> self. (692)

At the height of the Black Nationalist movement, LeRoi
Jones (now Amiri Baraka) wrote in "The Myth of a Negro
Literature" that "Negro" music is the only true form of art
American Negroes have produced because it is largely produced
by the underclass:

> [One] of the most persistent and aggravating reasons for
> the absence of achievement among serious Negro artists,
> except Negro music, is that in most cases the Negroes who
> found themselves in a position to pursue some art, espe-
> cially the art of literature, have been members of the
> Negro middle class, a group that has always gone out of
> its way to cultivate *any* mediocrity, as long as that medi-
> ocrity was guaranteed to prove to America, and recently to
> the world at large, that they were not really...Negroes.
> Negro music alone, because it drew its strengths and beau-
> ties out of the depth of the black man's soul, and because
> to a large extent its traditions could be carried on by the
> lowest classes of Negroes, has been able to survive the
> constant and willful dilutions of the black middle class.[5]

▲ ▲ ▲ ▲ ▲

Both Hughes and Baraka exemplify the way in which middle-class writers de-contextualize and "romanticize the folk," in Hazel Carby's terms. Neither writer acknowledges the complexity of working-class life; for each, the black working class is an autonomous space, free of negotiations with hegemony, that contains the pure source of musical and spiritual culture and inspiration. The black middle class, in contrast, is a space of pure compromise and capitulation, from which all autonomy disappears once it encounters hegemonic power.

In the late twentieth century, writers who have benefitted from integration and affirmative action—many of whom went to school in a predominantly white world but went home to a predominantly black one—have begun to critique the assumptions that underlie the exclusionary logic of authenticity discourse. By redefining the meaning of black middle-class experience, fiction writers such as Andrea Lee, Trey Ellis, Darryl Pinckney, Connie Porter, and Paul Beatty, and autobiographers such as Lorene Cary, Jill Nelson, Charlayne Hunter-Gault, Stephen Carter, and Jake Lamar explore how class position contributes to the construction of race and gender positionalities. While blackness may continue to be associated with victimization and the terms of that oppression vary widely because of class privilege, these writers show that class privilege does not carry with it a necessary betrayal of the race.[6] Rather than expanding the category of "real" blackness, they suggest that if all identities are discursively produced and under negotiation, then all identities are inauthentic.

In this chapter I examine three films released in 1991 that address issues around racial authenticity and the black middle class: *Livin' Large* by Michael Schulz, *Strictly Business* by Kevin Hooks, and *Ricochet* by Russell Mulcahy. The first two films are "new jack" comedies made by African-American directors; the third is a suspense film by a white Australian director. *Livin' Large* features largely unknown black actors, *Strictly Business* showcases moderately well-known younger black actors (Tommy Davidson and Halle Berry), and *Ricochet* is a vehicle for Denzel Washington and John Lithgow. Differences in style, tone, and address notwithstanding, these films are all fundamentally about the same subject: the political consequences of professional achievement for African-American males. In each case, a black man in the urban context is shown to pursue his own ambitions without sufficient regard for the condition of other black people. Each man's security (if not safety) is threatened by the effects of white racism and opportunism; each is saved professionally and reconstructed politically by his connection with an old friend from the neighborhood. None of these friends ("homeboys") has achieved the class status of the protagonists—they run the gamut from being unemployed, to working in a mailroom, to dealing drugs—but they have all retained their connections to a monolithically constructed black community; thus, they all stand for a communal ethos in contrast to the protagonist's individualism. As evidenced by their affiliations and their style of walking, talking, and dress, all are coded as being more "authentically black" than are the protagonists. By recognizing the knowledge and skill of his friend, each protagonist is saved from the destructive power of the state or the corporate elite. At the end of each film the protagonist is allowed to have it all—he reconnects with "the black community" and achieves even greater power and wealth.

These films all assume the existence of a particular type of black subject who is more authentic than any other; as such, they eschew the kind of self-questioning characteristic of the literary examples cited above. All enact the drama of racial authenticity, by which behaviors, attitudes, social relations, and commitments are evaluated based on the extent to which they represent or serve the interests of a romanticized "black community." Practices or beliefs that fail to meet this litmus test are designated as "not black," "white," inauthentic.

I

Theorists such as Thelma Wills Foote, Stuart Hall, Alycee Lane, Wahneema Lubiano, Kobena Mercer, Adolph Reed, Jr., Cornel West and others have persuasively outlined the limits of the discourse of authenticity.[7] First, under the sign of radical politics, the rhetoric of authenticity actually depoliticized the nationalist movements of the 1960s, because it silenced self-critique. In Reed's words, it "ruled out analysis of cleavages or particularities within the black population," replacing them with a romanticized, ahistorical, "obsolete, folkish model of black life." Secondly, as Reed further argues, it distilled black culture into its "commodity forms: ... red, black, and green flags; dashikis; Afro-Sheen; blaxploitation films; collections of bad poetry. (73-74) Third, it has typically relied upon constructions that equate blackness with misogyny and homophobia, by which feminists and gays and lesbians are coded as "not black." About this coexistence of an ostensibly progressive anti-racist position with misogyny and homophobia, Stuart Hall has written:

> ...certain ways in which black men continue to live out their counter-identities as black masculinities and replay those fantasies of black masculinities in the theatres of popular culture are, when viewed from along other axes of difference, the very masculine identities that are oppressive to women, that claim visibility for their hardness only at the expense of the vulnerability of black women and the feminization of gay black men. The way in which a transgressive politics in one domain is constantly sutured and stabilized by reactionary or unexamined politics in another is only to be explained by this continuous cross-dislocation of one identity by another, one structure by another.[8]

And fourth, the discourse of authenticity depends upon a logic which is ultimately self-contradictory. The rhetoric of racial authenticity is based on the apparent denial of racial essence. That is, it replaces a notion of racial identity based on heredity with one based on ideology. Ultimately, however, it deploys a constructionist argument in an essentialist manner for it uses racial and ideological positions interchangeably, designating as "white" or "non-black" anyone who departs from its positions on the grounds of class interests, gender, or sexual orientation.

The three films on which this chapter focuses belong to a genre that Henry Louis Gates, Jr. has called "guiltsploitation" pictures, since they require the protagonists to "pay" for their success. Although these films center on the dilemmas of middle-class black males, in their glorification of the urban underclass they resemble as well "new jack" dramatic pictures such as *New Jack City, Menace to Society, Juice,* and *Straight Outta Brooklyn.* Both types of films seek to recuperate a putatively authentic black subject. This may be the case because such figures gratify the desires of a mainstream audience for a black male outlaw, but as Gates has suggested, they may also provide a means by which black directors seek symbolically to reconcile themselves with the masses of black people whose political and class interests they fear are radically different from their own.[9]

My discussion of these films focuses on the way in which they construct the status of gender and race in the drama of class mobility, for each depends upon a spectacularization of racial and gendered identity that reduces race to style and reanimates timeworn conventions. Each plays out the narrative of the protagonists' changing class position in terms of his masculinity; none acknowledges the impact of changes in class position upon black women. This preoccupation with patriarchal power and authority compromises the films' apparent concern for the possibilities of change; each ultimately reinscribes a patriarchal, conservative agenda. Indeed, the static position of women only confirms the fundamental conservatism of these films which, to varying degrees, seek to recuperate the "American Dream" by suggesting it can contain and underwrite progressive, collective social transformation.

Livin' Large

Livin' Large is the story of Dexter Jackson, a young black man who rises from working as a deliveryman in his family's laundry business to starring as the anchorman on a network news team. To succeed as a newsman, however, he must shed his vernacular style of speech and hip hop wardrobe and manner in favor of a standard English mode of delivery and self-presentation. Within the film, the style he is required to assume is encoded as effeminized and therefore "white." As he becomes increasingly successful, he grows both alienated from his community and unable to resist the domination of the white woman for whom he works. Dexter reaches the point where he seems willing to renounce his personal desires altogether in order to succeed at the station. But he is saved by his own conscience and the love of the friends he has mistreated and is able to have both his racialized political identity and professional success.

Dexter is introduced to the viewer by his good friend, Baker Moon (Nathaniel "Afrika" Hall), who presents him within the context of their community on the east side of Atlanta. Baker describes Dexter as a man who has always dreamt of being an anchor man and "livin' large." As Baker talks, Dexter asks him to hold his video camera while he greets several people in the community, including the neighborhood barber and the owner of a local soul food restaurant. Dexter is thus framed doubly, in the film itself and in the demo he makes for a class assignment. The double framing highlights not only Dexter's career goals, but also his awareness of himself as spectacle and as commodity. At this point he seems to control his self-construction, but as we shall see, it is precisely the commodification of his own image that becomes the site of his struggles with hegemonic power.

A dark-skinned black man, Dexter is introduced in this opening sequence as a liminal figure. He is both deliveryman and friend to his customers. He is a "homeboy" like Baker but has higher aspirations than his friend does. And as the subject of Baker's narration, he occupies two narrative positions at once. He functions diegetically, appearing on camera and speaking to Baker and other characters; yet at times he also absents himself from the screen, providing Baker with an extra-diegetic subject. This liminality dramatizes the apparent contradiction between his aspirations and his connection with "the community."

Dexter is enrolled in classes at the Apex School of Broadcasting; his delivery on his videotapes suggests that he aspires to be a homeboy reporter, presenting news in street vernacular. Dexter happens to be on the scene when the local black anchorman is shot by a sniper; he seizes this opportunity to make his debut on network television. He takes the microphone and the camera up to the office in which the sniper has barricaded himself and persuades him to release his hostages and surrender to the police. Because Dexter's coverage of this event is a ratings success, the executive producer of network news, Kate Penndroggin (played by Blanche Baker) offers him a job as a reporter with the station. But quickly Dexter and his employer realize that they disagree about his job responsibilities. Kate insists that he lose his style, which is encoded in the film as "black." She works on his diction, requiring him, for example, to distinguish between "axe" and "ask." She expects him, as well, to dress more conservatively and to cut off his dreadlocks.

▲ ▲ ▲ ▲ ▲

Initially, Dexter hopes to use his spot to report on issues that concern his community. In his first story he shows how police response to emergency calls is determined by the racial and class demographics of the area from which the calls originates. When he reports from a working-class location in a voice that sounds "black" that five men are dead, the police never respond. But when he reports from a phone in a wealthy neighborhood that a woman may have twisted her ankle, a fleet of squad cars responds before he can complete the call.

Kate does not find this story sufficiently sensational or marketable. It is not enough for her that he change his personal style. To satisfy her sense of what the audience demands of African-American subject matter, he is expected as well to investigate not racism in law enforcement, but criminality within the black community, however petty. Thus, while Dexter begins by using mainstream media to speak for his community, he is forced to betray the secrets of his friends and neighbors in order to advance his career.

He returns to the ritual ground that established his character in the opening shots: Bubba's Barber Shop, Anna Mae's You'll Get Fat Soul Food Restaurant, and his friendship with Baker, and betrays each relationship in order to protect his own economic position. He exposes Bubba's numbers running operation and Anna Mae's high fat recipes. And when Baker tells him privately that Four Fingers Felix, a recently-paroled friend, is planning to rob an auto dealership, Dexter arranges for a camera crew to catch Felix in the act. Baker pays for his indiscretion by being beaten to within an inch of his life.

Even Dexter's intimate life is compromised in his rise to fame. His boss, Kate, does not find Dexter's girlfriend, Toynelle (Lisa Arrindell), sufficiently sophisticated, disapproving of her dress and her ability to dance, her speech, and her evident delight in Dexter's new-found wealth. Dexter allows himself to be seduced by Missy (Julia Campbell), the ambitious white "weathergirl," and is almost persuaded to marry her on network television to promote his ratings. During the televised ceremony he changes his mind. He exposes Kate's avarice to the viewing audience; Toynelle wreaks her revenge on Missy and Kate; and Dexter receives the anchor spot in return for his honesty.

The film clearly establishes an adverse relationship between the markers of black masculinity and professional success. As Dexter's career advances he becomes closer to Kate, more distant from Baker; thus, in the terms the film establishes, he sacrifices an important bond to his past for the sake of his connection to a white superior. Kate, the embodiment of hegemonic yet feminized culture over black autonomy, changes his speech, style of dress, hair, residence, and romantic interest. In turn, Dexter's desire for success allows him to surrender to the authority of this manufactured, video image of himself. The film not only suggests that he is becoming a less authentic black man—as he becomes increasingly accomplished, he loses his fluency in black vernacular and his ability to dance and to strut, moves to an apartment furnished entirely in white and almost marries Missy. But the film also encodes this capitulation as his literal "whitening." Whenever he watches a videotape of a broadcast in which he is personally or professionally compromised, he is confronted as well with the disruptive image of his alter ego, himself in white face, instead of his own dark-skinned image. This alter ego, an image of his subconscious fears of what he has become, appears with lips and nose that thin, skin that lightens, and hair that straightens each time he betrays a black person.

Once Dexter resists the tyranny of his artificially constructed media image and refuses to marry Missy, he is able to destroy his alter ego. By the end, in the terms the film establishes he is able to have it all. He has won Toynelle back. Moreover, he is able to co-anchor the news with the veteran male reporter he idolizes, and wears a dread fade and a vest of kente cloth on the air, signs, presumably, of his racial pride.

One would think that a film that can be summarized in this manner is concerned with exposing *both* the struggles over power and control waged in the realm of representation, and the contradictions between the interests of corporate America and those of the black underclass. Such an agenda would, however, presuppose that identity is negotiated within the realm of representation. As Hall writes:

> …[Rather than] thinking of identity as an already accomplished historical fact, which the new cinematic discourses then represent, we should think, instead, of identity as a "production," which is never complete, always in process, and always constituted within, not outside, representation.[10]

But by staging a struggle between the false, whiteface, video image of Dexter, and the "real" Dexter, the film suggests instead that there is such a thing as an authentic self that can be captured by the camera. Moreover, the staging of Dexter's real identity in the terms of dress, hairstyle, and hand gestures points to the commodification of authenticity to which Reed and Lubiano each refer. The problematic the film exposes is thus the inescapability of neither performativity, nor representation, nor hegemonic power. Rather, it cautions against surrender to the "wrong" performances, representations, or hegemonic controls.

One might argue that Dexter's escape from false representations into the real is called into question by the fact that we see him at the end of the film on camera with his co-anchor as he is watched (and cheered on) by his friends and family; his escape into the real might thus be read as provisional. However, the fact that Baker breaks the frame and speaks directly to the viewer as he did at the beginning seems to reassure us of the unquestionable authenticity and reliability of the working-class black man.

The positioning of black and white women in the film confirms the conservative gender politics at the heart of the discourse of authenticity that so many critics have identified. Toynelle and Missy are used only as static markers of the stages of Dexter's political and professional trajectory; Kate symbolizes the corrupt power of capitalism. The film is more concerned with re-establishing the bond between Dexter and Baker than it is with repairing that between Dexter and Toynelle. Moreover, when Kate, the symbol of hegemonic emasculation of black men, is purged from the station, black and white men are able to work together as symbols of state-sanctioned racial harmony in the urban context. A film that superficially offers a critique of conservative racial ideology, *Livin' Large,* thus reinscribes patriarchy in its demonizing of white women and its marginalization of black and white women from its central struggles.

Strictly Business

Strictly Business centers on a young black male character named Waymon Tinsdale (Joseph C. Phillips). An ambitious associate with a prominent commercial real estate firm in Manhattan, Tinsdale aspires to be a name partner. To accomplish this goal, he must close a big deal on a foreclosed high-rise, the Savoy Towers. Waymon's life and goals are contrasted with those of his homey, Bobby Johnson (Tommy Davidson), a mailroom employee who hopes to be appointed to the firm's management training program. As the film opens, Bobby is characterized as immature, lazy, and irreverent, but fun-loving and, most importantly, authentically black. While Waymon gets up before dawn

▲ ▲ ▲ ▲ ▲

to ride his stationary bicycle and prepare for the day, Bobby sleeps until the last minute and has to be rousted out of bed by the youngsters for whom his mother babysits.

At work, Waymon has a successful meeting with the Japanese investors to whom he hopes to sell the high-rise; Bobby is reprimanded by his supervisor for being late yet again. Over a business lunch later that day, Waymon sees and falls in love immediately with a sultry young woman named Natalie (Halle Berry), the host at the restaurant. Meanwhile, during the lunch hour, Bobby waits in Waymon's office to ask about getting a place in the training program. Showing his disgust for Bobby, Waymon criticizes him for being "too black;" Bobby accuses Waymon of being "straight up whiter than the whitest white man."

In his quest to learn more about Natalie, Waymon discovers that Bobby knows her from clubs they both frequent. Waymon promises to get Bobby into the training program if he will introduce him to Natalie. Bobby helps Waymon prepare for the club scene by showing him how to dress and talk "black." His first foray into the club is an embarrassment, but he does manage to win Natalie over.

To make room in his life for Natalie, Waymon has to rid himself of Deirdre (Anne Marie Johnson), his on again, off again girlfriend who believes herself to be his fiancée. Deirdre, who works in the corporate world, symbolizes the "white" phase of Waymon's life: she is high-strung, plays squash, has a mechanical approach to sex, and has mapped out their entire life. Natalie, who wears form-fitting clothing, walks sinuously, and is comfortable in black clubs, embodies black female sexuality. In this film, black women are thus clearly scripted into the discourse of authenticity.

Meanwhile, David Barnes, one of Waymon's white colleagues, jealous of Waymon's professional success, ruins Waymon's deal with the Japanese investors by tampering with the financial projections that Waymon had prepared for them. Waymon fires Bobby, who had taken the figures to the investors and appears at first to be responsible for the erroneous information. And Waymon's boss threatens to fire him if he is unable to find a buyer for the property. At the eleventh hour, Bobby unmasks David for the crook that he is and saves Waymon's career by producing a family of black male entrepreneurs, the Halloran brothers, who agree to purchase the property. Waymon not only guarantees Bobby a place in the training program, but he arranges for the Hallorans to buy Natalie her own club.

Like *Livin' Large, Strictly Business* displays a certain anxiety about the racial implications of class mobility. While the film does not offer an image of Waymon in whiteface, it does construct him as having lost touch with the behaviors and qualities associated with blackness and it codes that blackness in familiar terms of his gender identity and sexual prowess. Like Dexter, Waymon is shown to be unable to dance or to speak black vernacular when he is most fully identified with the corporate elite.

He is forced to recognize the inescapability of racism when the white man he believes to be his friend betrays him. The film ends with a heady, exuberant fantasy of black economic nationalism, in which capitalism provides the ground upon which racial solidarity and mutual respect between black and white men rest. Just as a hip hop cut provides the soundtrack to the closing images of *Livin' Large* where the interests of black and white men are reconciled, here too hip hop legitimates the final cross-racial male collaboration. The energy of the deal-making is intensified by the use of quick cuts showing the camaraderie between the brothers and the partners, and the use of Queen Latifah's cover of Gamble and Huff's "Money" on the soundtrack admonishing the listener not to "let money change you." The music in the sequences that end each film shows how resistance culture may be appropriated within hegemony in order to legitimate or authorize the status quo.

In contrast to the dynamism of the closing scenes of the film, women here too are locked into predictable positions. Here again, the black women are ancillary to the black man's political development. Deirdre, an extreme version of Waymon's conservatism, remains a virtual caricature of white middle-class womanhood. Natalie, on the other hand, never escapes her construction as a highly sexualized figure throughout the film. In the first scene in which she appears, she is shot first in slow motion, the camera panning up her body from Waymon's point of view. She wears a strapless dress and is shot at one point from mid-chest up to appear nude and vulnerable. By the end of the film we are meant to believe that she will be a successful entrepreneur, even though she is shown to have difficulty holding down a job. The club she receives at the end of the film is effectively a trinket tossed her way by the infinitely more powerful men who surround her.

Ricochet

Livin' Large and *Strictly Business* both foreground the issue of the politics of the black middle class directly. *Ricochet*, the only white-directed film of this group, focuses on a multitude of other issues, including the suspense plot involving the protagonist, Nick Styles (Denzel Washington) and his antagonist, Earl Blake (John Lithgow). But like the other two films, this one also turns on the protagonist's recognition that as a black man he cannot trust the legitimate (read "white") road to American success. His only safe haven is a cross-class alliance with the boys in the 'hood, even if they are gangbangers and drug lords.

Like *Livin' Large, Ricochet* is concerned as well with the spectacularization of the exceptional black man; much of the film is given over to other people watching Styles, Styles watching himself, and Styles being filmed or videotaped. The film suggests that Earl Blake is gay; his interest in consuming Styles's visual image covers the film's own fascination with Styles as an object of the gaze. As Elizabeth Alexander has put it, "The question of what it means to look directly, unabashedly, and with desire at black men from a number of subject positions is of paramount importance in considering this film. Styles participates in his own pornographizing."[11]

Ricochet focuses on Styles's meteoric rise from policeman and law student to assistant district attorney with his eyes on the mayor's office, the governor's mansion, and higher national office. The first two scenes provide defining moments in his career. In the first scene, he and Larry, his white partner, play basketball against Odessa (Ice T) and his associate, RC. Styles, Odessa, and RC have been friends since childhood, but while Styles has chosen a career in law enforcement, Odessa and RC are gang bangers and drug dealers. Styles is initially constructed in this scene as bicultural. He tells his white partner to stop playing like a white man; he and Larry are able to beat Odessa and RC because Nick can talk shit and slam dunk. However, as he accompanies Odessa to his Corvette, he realizes that the car is stolen and at that moment severs his connection to his "homeboy."

In this scene he stops to talk with a woman who has been watching the game and cheering him and Larry on. He asks her for a date and it becomes clear that Alice is the picture-perfect woman who will accompany him on his rise to power. From this point on, Alice functions to mark Styles's heterosexuality, appearing in the film only as the sign of her husband's progress on the path to middle-class respectability.

Styles's future successes are guaranteed in the next scene when he apprehends a white hit man, Earl Talbot Blake, in a sequence that a bystander captures on a home video camera.[12]

▲▲▲▲▲

Not only does Styles manage to wound Blake and take him into custody, but in an extended sequence, he voluntarily strips down to his boxer shorts in order to assure Blake that he is unarmed and persuade him to turn himself in. In this sequence, Blake has taken a young white woman hostage and hides behind her while holding a shotgun to her throat. After he has stripped down, Styles taunts him saying, "The only weapon I have now is useless unless you're a pretty girl." His words are both a sexual tease and a source of humiliation, aimed at a man who is hiding behind a woman's body even as he threatens her. Catching Blake off guard, Styles shoots him in the kneecap; when the video operator makes the tape available to network news, the scene of Blake's humiliation enters the arena of public consumption. Both in the hospital and in jail, Blake, haunted by his public humiliation, vows to avenge himself. He surrounds himself with visual images of Styles's rise to power, photographs of Styles cut from newspapers, xeroxes of those photographs, and eventually collages made of endlessly copied photographs cut into pieces.

The narrative of the film alternates scenes of Styles's professional success and family life with scenes of Blake's rise to power behind prison walls. Styles's success is the result of his ambition, intelligence, articulateness, compassion, and good humor. He is the perfect subject for the news footage, documentaries, and interviews through which the viewer frequently learns about him. In contrast, Blake builds his physical strength and beats his fellow prisoners into submission. As Styles pursues his pet project of raising funds for a children's center at the foot of the Watts Towers, Blake plans and executes a vicious, mass escape for himself and several members of the Aryan Brotherhood.

During the night of a telethon to raise money for the Towers Children Center, Blake's and Styles's paths cross again; at this point Blake seizes control of the plot of Styles's life and attempts to orchestrate his downfall. As visual representations of

Styles's career have documented his life as an American success, from this point on, Blake manipulates and fabricates media images of Styles so that to the popular imagination Styles becomes a pedophile, drug abuser, and adulterer.

This scene emphasizes the construction of Styles as media subject; the camera pans from a monitor at the telethon, to the telethon itself, before moving maniacally through the Styles home, capturing the daughters and their babysitter watching the telethon on television at home. The viewer is continually reminded of the fact that the media event and a new stage in Styles's career are being constructed as the event is taking place. While Styles and his father emcee the fund-raiser, Blake creates a power failure at Styles's home, poses as a repairman in order to get into the home, drugs the sitter, and installs a bug in the home. He had sent a $10,000 donation to the telethon along with an anonymous note; as Styles reads the note aloud at the telethon, the camera cuts away from the scene and pans through the Styles home as if looking for Blake. As the camera moves through the house, in a frenzy that mirrors Blake's delirious pleasure in looking at Nick's image, the viewer hears Nick's voice in the voiceover; eventually, the camera comes to rest in a high angle shot looking down on Blake watching Styles on a mini television.

After this scene, the power dynamic between Blake and Styles shifts. The next morning, Styles's closest associate, a black city councilman, is found dead, in leather drag, with a briefcase full of child pornography and a suicide note that implicates himself and Styles in acts of pedophilia. Blake and his sidekick then drug Styles and film him unwittingly having sex with a white woman. Blake overdubs an audiotape he had made previously of Styles's banter with a waitress. He has thus effectively created an alternative image of Styles which he then circulates on the network news. As a videotape had previously made his career, so this one threatens to destroy him. Because of

▲►▲▲▲►

this "evidence" of his indiscretion, Styles is suspended from his job; as Blake's sidekick remarks, Blake has singlehandedly "deconstructed" Styles's life in retaliation for what he believes was Styles's destruction of his own.

Meanwhile, Styles, recognizing that the plot of his life is being destroyed, breaks his own television and returns to Odessa, from whom he had earlier disassociated himself. He joins forces with him and the other homeboys in order to capture Blake and reclaim his good name. Styles had previously confronted Odessa in his crack house, warning him to stop dealing drugs and gangbanging at the center. In that earlier scene he accused Odessa and his followers of killing other black folks. But the resolution of the film turns on a blunt disavowal of that earlier moment. Suddenly, Styles finds that Odessa and the other boys from the 'hood are the only people he can trust and reassures his wife and children that they will be safer with Odessa and his men than they are with the police.

Their plot issues in an extended showdown between Styles and Blake, as a result of which Blake is electrocuted and impaled on a stake at the Watts Towers. As a newscaster reports near the end of the film, the scene provides violent and incontrovertible evidence of Styles's innocence. But while before, televised images had enabled Styles's successes, documenting the achievements for which he had been rewarded, he has seen them betray him and no longer trusts either the reliability of televisual evidence or the myth of American success to which it is so profoundly connected. The end of the film thus ironically rejects the power of the visual image. Styles's reunion with his family is played out against the background of a predictably sentimental soundtrack. However, that music is interrupted by a muted, but harsher hip hop beat as Styles renews his friendship with Odessa and promises to meet him on the asphalt on Saturday. The resistant and insistent beat of the soundtrack accompanies him over to the on-the-spot reporter who describes the scene for the News at Eleven audience. In contrast to his earlier eagerness to accommodate the media, now Styles refuses to comply with his own commodification. He remains on the margin of the frame, turns the camera off, and tells the reporter to kiss his ass. When he turns the television camera off, the screen fades to black. The image of a bullet explodes back at the viewer, and the soundtrack explodes into Ice T's rap, "Ricochet," a song about the violent relationships between black men and the police over which the closing credits roll.

Of the three films I've discussed here, *Ricochet* would seem to be the most subversive. First, it acknowledges explicitly the homoerotic tension between black and white males which remains implicit in the other two films. A paranoid or inverted biracial buddy movie, the film suggests the interdependency of black and white masculinities, and of narratives of possibility and limitation. The positionalities may be reversed, but the interweaving of Blake's and Styles's lives dramatizes the deep interconnections that link the two terms. (Indeed, Blake's obsession with looking at Nick stages the desire of the hegemonic viewer to own and master black bodies through the authority of spectatorship.) Secondly, it refuses to recuperate hegemony by avoiding the convention of lodging criminal behavior in a lone official. Third, it constructs representation as a practice that is both contaminated and unavoidable; Styles's only choice at the end of the film is to refuse the objectifying gaze altogether. The film suggests that to enter the realm of the visible at all, especially for a black man, is to be complicit with the violence of hegemonic culture.

Although *Ricochet* undertakes a critique of the state apparatus that is more rigorous than what we find in either *Livin' Large* or *Strictly Business*, the outcome of the film depends ultimately upon what is perhaps the most extreme romanticization of the black underclass. Styles overlooks his earlier censure of Odessa, a hardened criminal, and turns to him for help in the face of widespread betrayals. The film thus posits a sort of race loyalty than runs deeper than all other ties, and associates that bond with a communal knowledge capable of subverting any attempts to regulate black people's lives. Styles's associations with white culture occasion his downfall; his return to his roots provides his salvation. However fully the film appears to question the conventions within which it functions, *Ricochet* cannot emancipate Odessa from the realm of the "real."

I've examined here a set of recent films about African-American male professionals that display some measure of anxiety about class mobility. In each case, the protagonist both regains a sense of political responsibility to a monolithic black community and retains his wealth by re-establishing his bond with a homeboy. The utopian endings of each of these films allow the protagonists to have it both ways, but stereotypes about black and white women and the black middle- and underclass remain intact.

My intention here is not to recuperate representations of the black middle class. Rather, I am concerned to problematize the almost inevitable associations of the black middle class with assimilationism and racial betrayal, and the black underclass with racial authenticity and solidarity. These formulations leave both positions insufficiently examined. Moreover, in contemporary black film they depend upon the deployment and circulation of familiar behaviors typically encoded as "black" in mainstream cinema and television.

The multiplicity of films on this topic might constitute a response to the widening gap between the African-American underclass and their counterparts in the middle class. Or these plots may allow the middle-class filmmakers a means of justifying their own status by suggesting that they have not sold out the race. These films might suggest as well a heightened self-consciousness about the "price" of capital accumulation in the Reagan-Bush-Clinton years. However the present historical moment inflects the construction of black middle-class culture, the assumptions upon which this trend is based are familiar and longstanding; further exploration of these issues can, I think, productively illuminate some of the ways in which ideas about race, gender, and class circulate in contemporary culture.

Intersectionality and Experiments in Black Documentary

In this chapter I briefly sketch some ways in which the history of black-directed cinema and the history of African-American film criticism might be read as a search for an authentic black subject. I then discuss ways in which a group of self-reflexive documentaries and faux documentaries problematize this discourse and tradition by offering extended readings of Marlon Riggs's *Tongues Untied (1990)*, Cheryl Dunye's *She Don't Fade (1991)* and *The Potluck and the Passion (1993)*, Camille Billops's and James V. Hatch's *Finding Christa (1991)*, and Marco Williams's *In Search of Our Fathers (1992)*. Whether they centrally concern black gay men, black lesbians, black mothers, or absent black fathers, the documentaries on which I focus in this chapter sidestep issues of racial representativeness and accuracy or inaccuracy altogether and presuppose that black subjectivitiy is a site of contested negotiations. As texts on the boundary of fact and fiction that explore the tensions among constructions of race, gender, class, and sexuality, they lend themselves readily to an intersectional analysis of form, of content, and of relations between the two.[1]

I

D. W. Griffith's *Birth of a Nation* (1915), considered by many to be the symbolic, although not literal, origin of U.S. cinema, is frequently offered up by film historians as the inaugural moment of African-American cinema as well.[2] Based upon Thomas Dixon's bestselling novel *The Clansman* (1905) and authenticated by Woodrow Wilson's *History of the American People* (1902), *Birth*, the first feature length studio production, established fundamental codes of narrative film practice, and reproduced and circulated as truth for mass consumption the full range of black stereotypes for record-breaking audiences.

Michael Rogin details various ways in which Griffith sought to establish the historical accuracy of his film.[3] And not only was *Birth* constructed as conveying the truth about race relations in nineteenth-century U.S. culture, but it appeared as well to have had a direct impact upon contemporaneous race relations. Anti-racist individuals and organizations alike believed that *Birth*, released during the height of Jim Crow segregation and lynching, enhanced tolerance of racial—especially Klan—violence.

Thomas Cripps, Manthia Diawara, Ed Guerrero and others have argued that the images of African Americans found in *Birth*

▲ ▲ ▲ ▲ ▲

and reproduced throughout the history of U.S. cinema—types that run the gamut from indolent, subservient, buffoonish men and women to vicious black male rapists—have set the terms of black-directed narrative film. Black directors have historically considered such types to be negative and false representations of African Americans that have the potential to endanger the lives and circumstances of black people in the "real world." As a result, they have struggled to offer up alternative, positive, real or true representations of black life. To the extent that it seeks to replace false representations with "true" ones, the project of black film (and to some degree of black film criticism) might thus be read as the search for an authentic black subject or an authentic black cinematic practice.

This search has taken various forms, but an admittedly cursory overview reveals two dominant trajectories that recall debates about "Negro Art" that began during the Harlem Renaissance and persist until the present time. One strand, in which the authentic black subject is shown to be at least diligent and morally upright if not also refined and prosperous, is exemplified in early films such as The Colored Players Company's *The Scar of Shame* (1928), Oscar Micheaux's *God's Stepchildren* (1938), or a more recent work such as Gordon Parks's *The Learning Tree* (1968). These films offer up dramas about "respectable" black characters in order to counteract stereotypes of black lasciviousness and irresponsibility. The other strand, which provides cinematic contexts for cultural practices coded as authentically black—jazz, gospel, rootworking, religion, and so on—is exemplified by Spencer Williams's *The Blood of Jesus* (1941), *Go Down Death* (1944), and *Dirty Gertie from Harlem USA* (1946). As changes in the national economy since the 1970s have led to the de-industrialization and underdevelopment of urban centers and a decline in steady, decent-paying jobs for semi- and unskilled laborers, inner-city African-American communities have suffered disproportionately. It is thus not surprising that from the blaxploitation pictures of the 1970s through the new jack pictures of the 1990s, markers of drug and gang culture, rather than those of working-class life, have circulated and been read increasingly as signs of authentic black experience.

Several of the most commercially successful recent black-directed films—Spike Lee's *Do the Right Thing* (1989), Mario Van Peebles's *New Jack City* (1991), John Singleton's *Boyz 'N the Hood* (1991), and Matty Rich's *Straight Outta Brooklyn* (1991)—contain referents that gesture toward an externally verifiable "real life." Wahneema Lubiano has usefully problematized Lee's use of such markers—references to black vernacular culture—to encode his films as authentic black documents. Her observations about Lee's films might usefully be applied to Van Peebles's, Singleton's, and Rich's films as well.

She questions the way in which Lee and his work have been called upon to stand and speak for "the black community." This kind of fetishization, she argues, eclipses other kinds of oppositional cinematic work and insulates vernacularity from critique. As she puts it, "vernacular language and cultural productions allow the possibility of discursive power disruptions, of cultural resistance—they do not guarantee it."[4] The marketing of films such as these provides one way in which they are constructed as "real life." For instance, press kits for *Boyz*, *Brooklyn*, Joseph Vasquez's *Hangin' With The Homeboys* (1991), and Wendell Harris Jr.'s *Chameleon Street* (1989), recall the authenticating documents that accompany slave narratives. Repeatedly, we read that John Singleton grew up in South Central Los Angeles under circumstances similar to those experienced by Tre Styles, his protagonist; that Matty Rich grew up in the Red Hook housing projects in which his film is set and that he shot much of *Brooklyn* in his grandmother's apartment; that Vasquez grew up in the Bronx neighborhood in which *Homeboys* is set; and that the critically acclaimed but poorly distributed *Chameleon Street* is based on the true story of William Douglas Street. In short, most reviews of or feature articles on these films assure us of the authority of the directors' experience.

In contrast to the sanitized visions of contemporary urban life commonly circulated by mainstream Hollywood movies, these films contain markers of contemporary urban problems. To cite but one example, the opening credits of *Boyz 'N the Hood* unfold against the insistent, sinister whirring of police helicopters; the soundtrack is flooded with the sound of gunfire while the visuals are punctuated with flashing searchlights. Actual gangs are named, and characters wear clothing and colors appropriate to those organizations.

These films contain not only signifiers of gang and drug culture excised from images of the city in Hollywood films. They also contain markers that historicize and position them as interventions in the construction of a multi-faceted, contemporary, urban African-American culture of resistance. The markers locate the films in relation to black achievements in sports and music, and to ongoing cultural debates around constructions of race.

References to Mookie Wilson, Jackie Robinson, and Magic Johnson in *Do the Right Thing* recall popular black sports figures. These references simultaneously invoke the presence of teams with a history of comparatively progressive racial politics—the Mets, Dodgers, and Lakers—and indict by their absence their more intransigent counterparts: the Yankees and the Celtics.

The directors position themselves in a common enterprise with black musicians in the frequent use of hip hop in soundtracks, and with the visible presence of rappers on screen as actors. In the case of *Do the Right Thing*, Lee also uses what W. J. T. Mitchell calls a "musical Wall of Fame," a litany of the names of black rhythm and blues and jazz musicians.[5] By means of such markers, the directors locate their films in the context of cross-generic history of cultural resistance.

Furthermore, the visuals, dedications, and narratives place these films in relation to present-day debates around race, gender, sexuality, and economics. Graffiti on the wall of Sal's pizzeria names Tawana Brawley; the pizza parlor, baseball bat, and police chokehold are referents resonant with the stories of Howard Beach and Michael Stewart. It thus comes as no surprise that the film is dedicated to the families of victims of police brutality.

The problematic of interracial romance, as well as the geography of *Jungle Fever*, invoke a recent episode of racial violence; this film was dedicated to the memory of Yusef Hawkins. And *Boyz 'N the Hood* might be seen as intervening directly in the discourse around black males as an "endangered species." The techniques and narratives of these films thus conceal their status as mediations and suggest that they occupy an intimate, if not contiguous, relation to an externally verifiable reality.

Reviewers and certain viewers likewise grant these films a proximity to and power over real life that is rarely seen in discussions of other types of films. Perhaps the most salient example of this sort of conflation is evident in the panic that surrounded the release of *Do the Right Thing*. But law enforcement officers, theatre owners, and local merchants also voiced concern that the release of *New Jack City* and *Boyz* would precipitate gang wars. Thus the marketing of these films went beyond standard strategies of identifying target audiences and attempted to monitor the word and action on the street. In Los Angeles, for example, Columbia Pictures showed *Boyz* before audiences of Youth Gang Services counselors, social workers, politicans, psychiatrists, and police officers to ensure that young black viewers would understand that the film was not encouraging them to perpetrate destructive behavior.

The focus on "real world" consequences of black film presup-

▲ ▲ ▲ ▲ ▲

poses a direct, unmediated relationship between black viewers and black films. As Lubiano argues, this focus ignores both the complex processes of signification constructed within the films as well as the possibility of black critical engagement. And as Jacquie Jones also notes, the fetishization of these films eclipses other kinds of black-directed work currently being produced.[6]

I am especially interested here in the fact that among the crop of films that have been overshadowed by works such as those by Lee, Singleton, and Rich, are black-directed documentaries. On the one hand, one should not be surprised that black-directed documentaries enjoy only limited circulation, since non-fiction films in general are considered to be less commercially viable than fiction films. Given the interest of the general public in consuming "black life" through the medium of black film, however, one might expect that black documentaries, films that "show us situations and events that are recognizably part of a realm of shared experience," would enjoy particular visibility.[7]

II

Documentary has played a central role in the evolution of black cinema. Key figures in the development of black film such as William Greaves and St. Clair Bourne produced their early work in the television documentary format. And indeed, documentaries by Ayoka Chenzira, Warrington Hudlin, Michelle Parkerson, Debra Robinson, Carroll Parrott Blue, Carol Munday Lawrence, and others display the possibilities for the comparatively inexpensive and convenient techniques of the genre to preserve otherwise suppressed narratives for posterity.

Traditionally, documentaries that seek to supply missing stories or correct widely circulating misinformation have pretended to objectivity. Such realism is manufactured through a variety of fictional and cinematic techniques: narrative, juxtaposition, pacing, editing, framing, camera placement, etc. But documentarians typically work to naturalize these techniques or to render them invisible so as to avoid impeding the process of communication. And audiences typically accept the reality of what they see in documentary. Directors and audiences alike bracket questions of positioning, motivation, and audience, colluding in the knowledge that the presented testimony, albeit incomplete, is somehow "more real" than the silence or ignorance it purportedly counters.

In contrast, the films and videos on which I focus here frustrate viewers' formal and ideological expectations of both black cinema in general and of documentary in particular. They call into question viewers' desire to read their accounts as the authentic story behind the popular myths and misconceptions. Rather, each director destabilizes the medium and by so doing destabilizes as well both the specific subject and the more general idea of an authentic (black) subject. For instance, the black mother in Billops's and Hatch's *Finding Christa* is not the overly familiar, monolithic, transhistorical figure of nurturance and self-sacrifice that recurs in literature and film. Rather, Billops and Hatch locate the idea of black motherhood on a continuum: at one end stands the biological mother, who, for reasons having to do with her class position, community, and desires, chooses to give up her child. At the other end stands the adoptive mother who performs the traditional maternal function. The film prompts one to ask who the "real" mother is and indeed, how useful such a distinction actually is. Likewise, black lesbians in the films of Cheryl Dunye are not easily situated. Their sexuality is shown to be produced out of negotiations with white lesbians, with conventions of heterosexual pop culture performance and representational practices, as well as with other black lesbians.

▲ ▲ ▲ ▲ ▲

Tongues Untied

Although Riggs refers to *Tongues Untied* as a documentary, he also acknowledges the difficulty one faces in placing the work within a specific genre:

> [I call] *Tongues Untied* "experimental" video for lack of a better word. It crosses many boundaries of genre. It is a documentary. It's personal biography. It's poetry. It's music video. It's "vogue" dance. It's "vérité" footage of people just talking, speaking directly into the camera as if the camera is a person and the audience is right there. It's extremely provocative at times...it's humorous too.[8]

Indeed, inscribed within *Tongues Untied* is a tension between gestures toward and those away from documentary. The lines of poetry spoken in the voiceover at the beginning of the video establish the work in the familiar space of documentary by situating the untied tongues in opposition to pre-existing silences and distortions. And Riggs's autobiographical monologues might be said to provide the narrative structure of the video.[9] However, the diversity of voices in the work challenges easy attempts to read Riggs's experience as representative, or his account as authentic. This tension notwithstanding, I consider the work in the context of documentary films and videos because of its relation to a set of verifiable historical experiences, its organization around an overarching argument, and its positioning relative to pre-existing absences and distortions in representational practices.[10]

As exemplified in *Tongues Untied*, black gay male discourse exhibits profound connections to that of black feminism. As black feminists often position black women as the victims simultaneously of white racism and misogyny and black misogyny, so too are black gay men subjected to white racism and homophobia, and black homophobia. And as black feminism challenges the masculinism of the language of racial authenticity, so too does black gay male discourse challenge its homophobia.[11] As Kendall Thomas, Rhonda Williams, Alycee Lane, and others have shown, homosexuality has persistently been read as antithetical to authentic blackness on the grounds that homosexuality does not exist in "Africa," monolithically conceived; that its appearance among African Americans is thus a sign of their contamination by white cultural practices; and that two-parent heterosexual families produce the future generations and "strong" men that guarantee the survival of the race. In his powerful rejoinder to these claims, Thomas points to the "well-documented history of same-sex intimacy in diverse African societies." More importantly, he argues that this line of thinking deliberately distorts and denies "the convergent histories of racist and homophobic violence."[12]

The opening shots and sounds of *Tongues Untied* problematize notions of the authentic, presumptively heterosexual black man and stereotypes of black gay male style. The film begins with shots of a diverse range of African-American men (collegiate, Afrocentric, b-boys) in a variety of settings (a park, a city street, a basketball court). The unsuspecting viewer might well assume that these men are heterosexual, given their placement on the ritual grounds of African-American male culture. However, in the context of this video, unmarked male bodies and spaces are presumptively gay. Rather than constructing an overdetermined heterosexual black male identity, the panoply of black male subjects signal ways in which sexuality negotiates with constructions of race, class, and age.

The voicetrack at the beginning of the film likewise situates the black gay male subject within the broader community of black men ordinarily presumed to be endangered and heterosexual. In the voiceover, the phrase "Brother to Brother, Brother to Brother" repeats; incrementally, voices join the solitary voice with which the chant begins. The delivery of the line, and the poem that follows that line, together counteract the potentially isolated condition of the black gay male subject by subtly weaving black gay men into the discourse around black men in crisis.

The poem articulates the consequences of black male silence in response to racism. Only the use of the salutations "girlfriend" and "Miss Thang" early in the poem indicate that the speaker is gay. Otherwise, he identifies himself as black and male and recounts his response at being denied entrance to a jewelry store because the proprietor assumes he is a thief. The silence about which he speaks here recalls the familiar constructions of heterosexual masculinity:

> I will swallow that hurt, and should I speak of it,
> Will vocalize only the anger, saying,
> "I should have bust out his fucking windows."
> Some of the anger will be exorcised
> But the hurt which has not been given voice prevails
>   and accumulates.
> Silence is a way to grin and bear it ....
> I strive to appear strong and silent.
> I learn to ingest hatred at a geometric rate
> And to count silently to 10, 10,000, 10,000,000
> But as I've learned to mute my cries of anguish,
> So have I learned to squelch my exclamations of joy.

These lines are spoken over two sets of visual images: scenes of police violence against black men during an urban uprising, and a still photograph of a black man alternating with intertitles that refer to some of the major causes of black male victimization: racial violence, substance abuse, and AIDS.[13] Aurally and visually, then, the opening moments of *Tongues Untied* work to situate black gay men in relation to the struggles that face black heterosexual men as well.

In the sequence that follows, Riggs begins to undo the work of the opening sequence; he differentiates the circumstances of black gay men from those of their heterosexual counterparts. While previously he had shown men mostly in groups and suggested conditions that shaped the lives of all black men, here he performs on camera, nude, and alone, a dance sequence in which he seems to be defending himself from an attacker. The poem about silence spoken in the voiceover here emphasizes the emotional cost of voicelessness:

> Silence is my shield,
> It crushes.
> Silence is my cloak,
> It smothers.
> Silence is my sword,
> It cuts both ways.
> Silence is the deadliest weapon.

The admonition to end the silence is accompanied by the image of a black man kissing Riggs on the mouth.

Monologues about an automated gay dating service, two black gay men on a bus in Washington, D. C., racism in a black gay club, and the famous Snap!thology sequence introduce issues of black gay style and politics. However, Riggs's narration of experiences we presume to be autobiographical provides much of the structure of the film and dramatizes the process by which he felt himself become silenced because of his sexual orientation, race, and class. His description of his self-imposed isolation as a youth is intercut with voices hurling racist and homophobic epithets. The friendship and support of a young white male led to his preference for white lovers; however, his escape to San Francisco's Castro District forced him to confront the racism of the '70s gay scene.

He says he "quit" the Castro in search of someplace better.

▲ ▲ ▲ ▲

The scenes that follow suggest that that place is "the black community," for here ballads by Roberta Flack and Nina Simone accompany slow motion sequences that focus on black drag queens. But these nostalgic, romanticized moments are quickly undermined by the voices of black homophobia, most notably exclusionary, religious rhetoric, pop culture ridicule, and pro-family nationalist ideology.

Up until this point, Riggs himself appeared on camera and spoke the lines we read as autobiographical. By intercutting these utterances with racist and homophobic epithets, he performs the way in which public discourse silences and shames minoritized identities. The scenes that follow the slow motion ballad sequence primarily expose and critique black homophobia. Constructed similarly to the earlier scenes that feature Riggs, they nevertheless contain significant differences. First, not Riggs, but the late writer Essex Hemphill appears on screen as the organizing, authoritative subject. Second, while Riggs speaks in the earlier sequence, here we confront the voiceless image of Hemphill, motionless except for his eyes that flicker with the pain of suppressed rage. While he is on camera, various speakers utter lines about silence, rage and repression. Only after the battle between the off-camera voices of closeted gay identity and the on-camera voices of black homophobia has reached a fever-pitch, does Hemphill himself speak on camera. His affirmation of black gay male rage constitutes an important shift in tone and point of view in the work.

In his narrative, Riggs describes his movement from anger and silence to a bold acceptance of his racial and sexual identities. However idealized the rhetoric around following "the beat of his own heart" may seem at first blush, that tone is, of course, shaped profoundly by the other rhythm, "the time bomb ticking in [his] blood," and in the blood of his brothers, the scores of black men whose faces jockey for position on screen with his own.

▲ ▲ ▲ ▲ ▲

The ending of *Tongues Untied* echoes the tone of its beginning. As the video opens with images that link the circumstances and struggles of black gay men to those of their heterosexual counterparts, it ends with a similar gesture toward connecting the agenda of the black gay movement with that of other African-American struggles for liberation. While in the beginning scenes gay men might be read as passing, here there is no confusing their sexual identities; footage from Civil Rights demonstrations is crosscut with that from a Gay Pride March.

Alycee Lane rightly questions whether the return to the ritual ground of black liberation actually re-inscribes the discourse of authenticity which the film critiques. Riggs may well appear to argue that black gays "are too black"; that is, that they have as much right to lay claim to blackness as do other black people. But the final gesture might also be understood to explode the notion of the authentic black subject, since it expands the category to include not only those who are gay, but also those who love interracially.

Riggs's last film, the posthumously completed and released *Black Is ...Black Ain't* (1995) revisits tensions and concerns central to the earlier work. If *Tongues* explores what it means for black gays and lesbians to lay claim to blackness when that discourse is synonymous with heterosexuality, *BIBA* speaks simultaneously to the paradoxical but fiercely urgent nature of this issue. The search for home and community drives the film, despite its skepticism, because, in Riggs's words: "The connection between AIDS and black folks and black folks' death isn't metaphorical. Both of them are a struggle against the odds in the face of adversity, in the face of possible extinction."

And indeed, the pall of death and loss weighs heavily in this work: people are dying while the issue of who is black is being debated. Archival footage from the Civil Rights and Black nationalist movements and family photographs not only situate

▲ ▲ ▲ ▲ ▲

the struggle for gay visibility and acceptance within black cultural history and black family narratives. They also establish a tone of nostalgic yearning that, as Riggs says of the song "To Be Young, Gifted and Black," "provokes painful memories of innocence," for a generation that once believed in the infiniteness of its own aspirations and possibilities.[14] Moreover, viewers know that Riggs died making the film; footage of Riggs's physical decline as he lies in his hospital bed or moves through various scenes is woven into the central narrative of the film. His spectral form struggling to continue to work, to provide the explanatory voiceover, underscores his sense of the cost of exclusionary practices and the consoling value of home.

Through a striking range of voiceovers and on-camera interviews, the film provides a sense of the many ways in which blackness has been defined and understood throughout history, taking particular note of how the '60s and '70s rhetoric of racial pride eased some of the pain of racial self-loathing. And yet, the militancy of this position established certain racial litmus tests by which many found themselves excluded from this imagined community on the basis of their politics, sexual preferences, language, class, education, etc. Thus even as the film celebrates the value of black community, it also critiques the strategies by which it polices its members.

Skeptical intertitles, and voiceovers of cultural studies theorists such as bell hooks, Michele Wallace, Barbara Smith, and Cornel West challenge the idea of a monolithic black community. Nevertheless, the film struggles to situate and celebrate blackness in a multiplicity of cultural practices and institutions—religion, food, music, dance, oratory, etc. For it is in the embrace of an imaginary black community that Riggs's outcasts long to rest.

▲ ▲ ▲ ▲ ▲

She Don't Fade and *The Potluck and the Passion*

Cheryl Dunye's *She Don't Fade* and *The Potluck and the Passion* resist categorization as documentaries even more fully than does *Tongues Untied*.[15] I consider these works in the documentary context for a variety of reasons. As is the case with *Tongues*, they perform some of the work of documentary: their very existence addresses gaps and distortions in pre-existing media representations. By making lesbian lives visible—sexual activity as well as the common social arrangements of life and work—*Fade* and *Potluck* respond both to mass cultural representations of lesbians as "perversely and exclusively sexual," and lesbian representations that downplay sexuality to accommodate "the heterosexual world of dominant culture."[16] Further, vérité techniques and the use of talking heads that comment on the action and situations are at least as representative of documentary as they are of fiction film techniques. Moreover, Dunye's refusal to separate diegetic from extra-diegetic material in both works blurs the boundary between fact and fiction; if they document nothing else, they seem to document certain aspects of the filmmaking process. And finally, the plot connections between *Fade* and *Potluck* suggest the existence of an extra-cinematic reality to which the two works point. While the videos flirt with their relation to a set of externally verifiable events, neither clarifies that relation; thus, the very indeterminacy that prompts me to consider these works documentaries could well justify calling them fictions. For the purposes of this argument, then, I categorize them as mock- or pseudo-documentaries.[17]

She Don't Fade centers on a character named Shae Clarke, played by Dunye herself, who is on the lookout for a new lover. Having just ended the last in a series of monogamous relationships, Shae tries a new approach, hitting on women she finds attractive wherever she happens to meet them. Her first attempt fails. Her second, with a woman named Margo, succeeds temporarily; they have a date, make love, seem to begin a relationship. But Shae breaks up with Margo when she sees and is attracted to Nikki. At the end of the video, Shae and Nikki meet at a party, discover their mutual attraction, and, as one of their friends says to the camera: "the rest, girls, is history—I mean herstory."

The straightforwardness of this summary belies the ironic relation the film has to its content. *She Don't Fade* is as much about issues surrounding black lesbian representation as it is about its ostensible plot.

The first thing we see after the opening credits might be read as a prologue. The director introduces herself and her subject and tells us that she plays the protagonist in the film. This monologue obscures as much as it reveals, for it offers and then withholds the legitimating authority of experience we expect from documentary. First, the shift in pronouns makes it unclear whether Cheryl is talking about herself or talking about Shae. She begins:

> Hi. I'm Cheryl and in this video I play Shae Clarke. Um. Shae's 29 years old. She recently broke up with a lover, about a year ago, and around that time she started her own vending business which is really really good. It's a good business...You meet a lot of people. You're out on the street. You're really self-engaged. It was good to do that at that time because it, you know, got me into myself when I'd been in relationships with women consecutive [sic]. This last one was three years. The one before that was so many years. I'd been going out with women pretty much as a livelihood for a while.

The shift to the "you" signals a break in the strategy of address. The "you" seems to suggest a heightened intimacy with the viewer, but it also hints at the speaker's familiarity with the experience of which she speaks. The implication that Cheryl is talking about herself might be confirmed by the shift from second person to first. But since we aren't certain how we are to read the change in pronouns, we are likewise unclear as to how we ought to read the shift in the tone and pace of her delivery, a shift which seems on the face of things to suggest that she's describing her own life. In short, this prologue, which may or may not be an extra-diegetic moment, marks only the inscrutability of signs of authenticity in the work.

The next sequence further transgresses the boundary that separates the two sides of the camera. The off-screen voice of Cheryl/Shae asks a woman she sees on the street and who is visible to us on screen, if she will allow herself to be interviewed for a video on women. Cheryl/Shae tells the woman she has "the look" she wants, a line to which the woman responds with some skepticism before walking away. We ask ourselves here if this Cheryl has entered the role of Shae and is thus performing her new approach, or if Cheryl, speaking in her own voice, is using the video to pursue her own agenda.

Additionally, the scene mocks the notion that a film can get at "real" lesbian experience by highlighting the role of performance in sexual pursuit. Indeed, in that regard, sexual pursuit and documentary film occupy similar terrain. For to be effective, sexual pursuit and documentary film alike require the subject to "act naturally" enough for the spectator to suspend disbelief willingly.

Throughout the video Dunye parodies conventions of representing romance and eroticism in order to undermine viewer desire for sincere and authentic images. Her use of outtakes dismantles the notion of the authoritative, explanatory voiceover. Likewise, any inclination on the part of the viewer to mystify sex is undermined by the critique that crew members offer Shae and

Margo during a sex scene. Elsewhere, Dunye's parodic performance of "Torn Between Two Lovers" mocks the way in which popular music contributes to the production of feeling and appropriates for her own purposes the sentimentalization of heterosexual romance.

Her refusal to distinguish between director and character, her inclusion of outtakes, and her parody of the conventions of erotic representations, enable Dunye to challenge viewer expectations that her narrative will provide them with the "real" black lesbian story. Rather, by calling attention to a range of fictionalizing techniques that produce the illusion of reality, Dunye mocks viewer expectations of documentary sincerity and constructs a lesbian subject in process and under negotiation.

At first glance, *The Potluck and the Passion* appears to be a sequel to *Fade*; it opens with the Nikki and Shae characters from *Fade* planning a dinner party on the occasion of their first anniversary. However, here too the relation between "reality" and the world of the video is quickly destabilized; Shae (Dunye) is here called Linda, and Nikki is never named.

While the self-reflexive moments in *Fade* highlight the technical aspects of the cinematic process, in *Potluck* such asides emphasize instead certain of the work's ideological assumptions. On several occasions, the narrative is interrupted by actors stepping out of their screen character and into a role that feels like their off-screen "character" to address the viewer about some aspect of the role they perform. Each of these digressions concerns the intersectionality of race and sexuality.

For example, in the first section, called "Homoplace," Linda and her lover's unnamed black gay male friend and neighbor (played by Robert Reid-Pharr) claims ownership over the meanings that attach to terms such as "queen," "gay," and "black," words that at other times and in other contexts have been considered derogatory.

▲ ▲ ▲ ▲ ▲

Reid-Pharr stops by to help Linda and her lover prepare for the potluck but declines to stay because the guest list: "Too much fish on the menu," he says. He walks in while Linda gives directions to Lisa and Kendra over the phone and her lover dusts, asks if they plan to clean up, and tells them that their flowers are "wrong." He subsequently offers to help Linda's girlfriend get dressed and to wrap the anniversary gift she has bought.

To anticipate any reading of his behavior as merely clichéd or stereotypical, *Potluck* cuts away from the scene in the apartment to three shots of Reid-Pharr's character speaking directly to the camera. Twice he simply says the word "queen," as if to punctuate or comment on the scene that has gone before. But the third time he actually analyzes his use of the term, saying that the word need not signify an end to conversation or the reducing of character. For him, it functions like the term "black," which need not be read necessarily as a closing off of possibilities. Rather, he argues, terms like black, queen, butch, and femme that have been used to limit or denigrate social positions might be reappropriated to read expansively. He remarks that his character wouldn't feel that the term "queen" reduces him.

This digression not only complicates *Potluck*'s strategies of address, situating the work in ongoing debates about performance, representations, and discourses about and within minoritized communities. It also links the work to documentary practice, for it allows Reid-Pharr, a theorist of race and sexuality and English professor at Johns Hopkins University, to function as the voice of the authoritative commentator.

Much of the action of *Potluck* focuses on the reconfiguration of relations among three of the guests at the dinner party: Megan, Tracy, and Evelyn.[18] Megan, who is white, and Tracy, who is black, have an uneasy dating relationship. Indeed, during the course of the film it becomes clear that while Megan believes they have a relationship, Tracy does not. At the party, Tracy meets Evelyn who is, like her, a black woman from the Washington, D. C. area. As the two women talk, their mutual attraction becomes unmistakable and Megan begins to feel jealous and displaced. She eventually storms out of the party, leaving Tracy and Evelyn together.

The tensions among these three women suggest complex interactions between race and sexuality, as well as issues of black and lesbian authenticity. Megan, a graduate student in English at Rutgers specializing in African-American literature, wears her anti-racist and sexual politics like a badge. She has worked as a Peace Corps volunteer in Ethiopia so she can "understand the problems of the Third World," and boasts about her disruptive behavior in an ACT UP demonstration in Washington, D. C.

In her talking head digression, the actor who plays Tracy (and identifies herself as Shelita) is concerned that Megan's interest in her is grounded in a need to legitimate her own progressive politics and showcase her knowledge of black culture. While she was first impressed and a little chagrined by the fact that Megan knows more about African-American culture than she herself does, Tracy has come to resent feeling displayed. To her mind, for Megan, knowing the other is tantamount to owning that other; her liberal impulses slide all too easily into colonizing gestures. And indeed, in one of her digressions, Megan (who says that her name is Nora) admits that her character was wrong to think that she had control over Tracy.

Tracy's and Megan's commentaries initially punctuate the action of the film in the way that Reid-Pharr's do. But in a couple of instances, the camera cuts from one digression to the other so that a debate between the characters/actors is interpolated into the narrative of the film. Moreover, in the digressions, Nora and Shelita perform their discomfort, anger, and disappointment to such good effect that they would seem to bring the authority of experience to their role as commentators.

▲ ▲ ▲ ▲ ▲

Perhaps because she feels that she has just failed an authenticity test, Tracy, a Rutgers graduate student specializing in the nineteenth-century Irish novel, becomes defensive when Linda (a graduate student in African-American Studies) asks her if any black people wrote novels during the period she studies. Tracy's facial expression signals her rejection of the implied assumption that she should "do" black people (pun intended) because she is black.

But Tracy is not the only person whose identity politics come under scrutiny. Tracy seems initially to be threatened by the ease with which Evelyn speaks about her racial and cultural politics and affiliations. And Megan questions her "lesbian credentials," after Evelyn speaks of Tambo, a man she once loved. However, Tracy and Evelyn soon acknowledge their attraction to each other and contempt for Megan, and the video ends with the suggestion that a new relationship is about to begin.

While on the surface the narrative may thus seem to be merely "a comic soap opera," the mock-documentary digressions call attention to the way in which even lesbian romantic comedy is read and consumed as corrective and explanatory. Moreover, they position the film within the discourse that critiques racial authenticity. The explicit coding of the racial and sexual identities of Dunye's characters is not contingent upon their ability to pass one kind of litmus test or another. The interplay of race and sex makes clear that their lives and positionalities are too complex and unpredictable to reduce to easy answers. To borrow Reid-Pharr's formulation, race and sex become the places where conversations begin, not where they end.

Finding Christa

If the style of *Tongues Untied, She Don't Fade,* and *The Potluck and the Passion* presupposes an insufficiency of material by and about black gays and lesbians, Billops's and Hatch's *Finding Christa* responds to the surfeit of material about black motherhood. For if black lesbians are virtually invisible in visual culture, the black mother—long-suffering, eternally nurturant, and self-sacrificing—is all too available for mass consumption.

Billops and Hatch, her co-director, de-mythologize the idea of "the black mother" in their account of Billops's decision to give up her four-year-old daughter for adoption and the reunion between the two women twenty-one years later. Additionally, they deploy a range of strategies to resist the voyeurism of camera and spectator alike. Through their use of dramatic reenactments, pantomime, and dream sequences they underscore the performative nature of representations of sincerity. Billops as subject thus refuses to gratify spectatorial desire for the classic payoffs both of documentary film and of sentimentalized black maternity—the tear of remorse or recognition and the disclosure of deep feeling.

Finding Christa opens with a photograph of the four-year-old Christa as she appeared shortly before Billops gave her up. The adult Christa speaks in a plaintive voice that reveals her sense of longing and betrayal: "My last memory of you is when you drove off and left me at the Children's Home Society. I didn't understand why you left me. I felt so alone. Why did you leave me? It's been so long since I felt complete."

In the dramatic reenactment that immediately follows, Billops plays a tape she has received from Christa in the Manhattan loft she shares with Hatch. She explains to her friend Corinne, who listens to the tape with her, that "I was trying to give her something else, because I felt she needed a mother and a father. I'm sorry about the pain it caused Christa as a young child, but I'm not sorry about the act."

The film then takes viewers back to the community in Los Angeles where Billops and her family lived and where she made

▲ ▲ ▲ ▲ ▲

her choice. Clips from home movies taken at Billops's baby shower and still photographs of Christa being bathed and playing under the Christmas tree recreate the apparent joys of this ostensibly perfect '50s family. However, interviews with friends and relatives confirm Billops's account of the limited options available to single mothers at the time.

The reasons behind Billops's choice are as complex as the assortment of voices that contribute to the film. From the testimonies, we learn that Billops gave Christa up because she did not think that she would be a good mother; she lacked sufficient family support; and she wanted to develop her talents as a visual artist. Her cousin Bertha believes she gave up Christa to be with Hatch, who is white and whom she married years later.

Up to this point, the film relies upon conventional documentary techniques: archival footage, interviews, and still photographs performed by playwright George C. Wolfe, Billops, and Christa. But here, the film moves into what Barbara Lekatsas calls a "surreal theatrical interlude."[19] In this sequence, Wolfe plays the role of the emcee in a mother-daughter recital for which Billops is auditioning. Dressed childishly in a frilly white dress with a blue sash, and wearing a feather boa, Billops attempts unsuccessfully to lip-synch to her own voice yodelling on the soundtrack while a pianist, seated behind her, accompanies her. As Billops takes her bow and turns to thank the pianist, she discovers to her horror that the accompanist is her daughter.

This dreamlike sequence enacts obliquely the complex feelings of alienation and dislocation Billops experiences but will not speak. Auditioning alone for a mother-daughter recital, dressed in a child's dress, and unable to match her lip movements to the music, Billops performs her anxiety about playing a predetermined role. These concerns notwithstanding, in the voiceover that follows Billops announces her decision to let Christa visit.

▲▲▲▲▲

While the first section of the film focuses on Billops's story, the second centers on Christa's life after she was left at the Children's Home Society. Through interviews with Christa, her adoptive siblings, and adoptive mother, Margaret Liebig, we learn that she found what appears to be a nurturing family. A singer, Liebig encouraged Christa's love of music. Despite this level of support, Christa is clearly haunted by deep dissatisfactions. While she is a bit more self-revealing than Billops is, her anxieties are also played out primarily though pantomime and staged home video sequences.

With Margaret's encouragement, Christa and Billops meet. But the reunion is not idealized. In the reenactment and theatrical interlude which follow, mother and daughter share family photos and accounts with no small degree of resentment and hostility.

In *Finding Christa*, Margaret conforms more closely to the type of the black mother than does Billops. Margaret approximates the physical as well as the emotional type; she weeps almost immediately, is physically affectionate, and slips easily into inflections and asides commonly associated with black maternal vernacularity. She can be seen to provide the comfort zone of identification which Billops as character refuses to supply. One might be tempted to say that she functions as the authentic black maternal voice in the film. I would suggest instead that the construction and placement of her character and the responses she invokes prompt us to scrutinize our own investments in the narrative and emotional weight of black maternity.[20]

Thus the visual style of *Finding Christa* complements its themes and convictions. The interweaving of interviews and archival footage presents one set of facts, but truths too intimate for direct testimony, too private for the spectatorial gaze, are encoded in the hallucinatory interludes. Moreover, the striking contrast drawn between Christa's two mothers undercuts any monolithic notion of Black motherhood.

▲ ▲ ▲ ▲ ▲

In Search of Our Fathers

Marco Williams's *In Search of Our Fathers* tells the story of the director's nine-year search to find his father. Just as Billops uses her own circumstances to reflect upon the hypervisibility of black mothers in *Finding Christa*, in *Fathers* Williams situates his personal history in relation to widely circulating myths of absent African-American fathers and the dysfunctional families they leave behind. Sociological and cultural analyses of black life in the United States (à la Moyers and Moynihan, to name just two) blame crises in African-American communities on absent black fathers and single black mothers. Such studies fail to acknowledge not only the impact of broader social and economic factors upon African-American lives but also the misogyny of their assumptions. They fail to recognize, in other words, the inescapable presence of constructions of gender in the discourse of race and class.

In *Fathers*, Williams critiques the relentless masculinism of these narratives about the crisis of black manhood. Without falling into the trap of romanticizing single-parent households, Williams challenges the assumption that matrifocal families are pathological. Through interviews and the voiceover we return with Williams to the home of his extended family in Philadelphia, where successive generations of women raised children without husbands. Perhaps because of the network of nurturing relatives, as one of his cousins says, their family is "proof that women raising children without fathers doesn't breed delinquents."

Indeed, Williams would seem to offer his own and his mother's story as a powerful counterexample to familiar mainstream representations of black single-parent households. Although Winnie, his mother, dropped out of college to give birth to her son, she does not seem to have sacrificed much in the way of mobility and independence: she went on to a career in banking in New York before moving to Paris to become a chef de partie. When we meet up with her near the end of the film, she is living in Cambridge, Massachusetts. Williams himself is also ambitious. A Harvard alumnus, he is enrolled in the film school at UCLA by the time he completes *Fathers.*

Like Billops and Hatch, Williams prompts those to whom he speaks to discuss issues that have long been shrouded in silence. However, more explicitly than Hatch and Billops do, Williams constructs his film to be a corrective account to popular cultural representations. In an early voiceover that accompanies a vérité sequence, for example, he alludes to sociological reports commonly understood to be true that pathologize the black family. No dramatic reenactments or surreal interludes here, most of the film is given over to conventional techniques of documentary filmmaking such as interviews and still photographs that establish the objectivity of the directorial perspective. The film might thus be read as seeking to replace popular "negative" images with "positive" ones.

However, Williams incorporates a variety of self-reflexive gestures in the film that allow him to avoid the trap of this kind of binary thinking and undercut his authority. These reminders call attention to the artificiality of mainstream and oppositional representations alike. While these inclusions may be read as disingenuous markers of the filmmaker's humility before the power of his medium, they might also be seen to undermine the illusion of cinematic transparency that naturalizes and authenticates partial truths.

The most fascinating interviews in the film are those Williams conducts with his father and his mother. They compel us not only because of what they suggest about gender and parenting, but also because of what they reveal about the process and ethics of documentary filmmaking. The film begins with a taped phone conversation between Williams and his father, James Berry, during Williams's senior year at Harvard. During this conversation, Williams attempts to set up a meeting with the reluctant Berry and announces to him both that he wants to make a film about their relationship and that he is recording their exchange. Clearly annoyed by these revelations, Berry refuses to consent to a process he considers "surreptitious" and "counterproductive."

By beginning the film in this manner, Williams opens up for scrutiny the complex power relations between documentary film-maker and subject. He is both participant and observer in this nar-rative; while the investments that attend each position sometimes run in tandem, they also sometimes oppose each other. Williams the private citizen may need to meet his father to gain information and satisfy some personal longing, but Williams the filmmaker knows that he is sitting on a timely and marketable narrative. The private citizen may wish to interrogate his father in order to pun-ish him, but the filmmaker needs to maintain cordial relations. The filmmaker may seem merely to turn his camera upon an experi-ence in order to make it available to the viewing audience. But the transparency and apparent objectivity of his position are belied by the editing techniques and use of sound that inflect each position emotionally and politically. In this sequence, Williams's use of a poignant soundtrack emphasizes his feeling of abandonment. However, he also signifies on his father's obvious class aspirations by including his halting use of multisyllabic words.

The conversation we overhear is both a private and a public event, although at the time the exchange occurs, only one par-ticipant is aware of that fact. Berry's anger at this revelation exposes Williams's position as intermediary: we cannot escape the fact that his search for the "real" story implicates us in a voyeuristic relationship with his father. From this opening sequence, we cannot avoid recognizing the questionable ethics both of documentary looking and making. The authenticity of this cinematic practice is thus challenged by the construction not only of the subject, but of the director as well.

Throughout *Fathers*, Williams makes futile attempts to speak with and visit Berry; finally, nine years after the film begins, the two men meet at Berry's home in Ohio. So much has led up to this meeting that this scene clearly constitutes the film's climactic encounter. As Williams acknowledges after the conversation, meeting his father is disappointing and has no real effect upon him: whatever his expectations, the encounter hasn't "changed [his] life" or "made him whole." Although Berry eventually warms to Williams, he is unmistakably crude and insensitive; in retrospect, Williams is relieved that he did not have to sustain an ongoing relationship with him. The meeting certainly challenges the masculinist assertion made earlier in the film that boys need "a man image" in the family while they're growing up.

Although the film centers on the search for Berry, Williams's conversations with Winnie, his mother, reveal much about the director himself; they too comment interestingly about the subtleties of the documentary process. During the course of the film, Williams travels first to Paris, then to Cambridge to visit and talk with Winnie. These conversations are skillfully edited to reveal how mother and son work through their discomfort with both the subject of Williams's conception and the presence of the camera. In the initial exchanges with his mother, Williams rarely appears on camera; his is a disembodied voice that asks intrusive questions that she tries to avoid. By the end of the film, they appear on camera together and each questions and responds to the other. The evolution of their onscreen relationship suggests the depth of the bond that connects them and subtly overturns the presumptively masculinist narrative of black men in crisis.

The moments of self-reflexivity occur at key points during his exchanges with Winnie. Twice while he visits her he includes slates (places that mark the synchronicity of soundtrack and visuals) to call attention to the presence of the camera. These moments disrupt the illusory seamlessness of the cinematic practice and highlight the awkwardness of the structure and content of the interview. Viewers may feel more sympathy for Winnie than we do for Berry; nevertheless, we stand in voyeuristic relation to both of them.

Later in the film, on two separate occasions, first the tape recorder malfunctions, then the film runs out. The tape recorder breaks as Winnie describes a fantasy she had while pregnant of falling down a flight of stairs and losing her baby; Williams runs out of film during the final moments of his last conversation with her. Clearly, he could have chosen to edit both of these moments out of the film. But by leaving them in, he de-mystifies his role and power as director. He acknowledges the partial nature of the counterargument to which the film points. Perhaps most significantly, he allows Winnie room to exceed the limiting gaze of the voyeuristic spectatorial gaze.

Bill Nichols, Linda Williams, E. Ann Kaplan, Trinh T. Minh-ha, and others have suggested that alternative documentary films and videos commonly point to their own fictionality in order to problematize widely circulating ideas about the nature of truth. To the extent that this is true, the works discussed here can be said to participate in a wide-ranging cultural project more easily than they would appear to re-define the nature of black documentary. But if black film and black bodies are expected to meet the test of realness—thus bearing disproportionately the burden of authenticity—I would suggest that the directors' refusal of claims to reality has particular implications for the ways in which black subjectivities are constructed.

Riggs, Dunye, Billops and Hatch, and Williams raise a series of important questions about race, representation, and discourses of authenticity. They eschew the impulse to use the documentary form to tell "positive," "true" stories in respond to the partial accounts that circulate in mainstream media, pointing instead to the inevitable limitations of their medium. Moreover, rather than showcasing nuclear, "in tact" families in response to prevalent accounts of pathological black families, they complicate notions of black mothers, fathers, communities, and households. Perhaps most importantly, they problematize the ethics of documentary looking and the limitations of spectatorship itself as a process of learning through looking. Given the extent to which the spectacularization of the bodies of people of color has served the interest of hegemony, they suggest that documentary looking at others, even with the most noble of intentions, may well be fundamentally indistinguishable from the voyeurism by which the bodies of people of color have long been fetishized and controlled.

Convergences:
4/29/92

this project developed out of my interest in exploring how the theory of intersectionality functions in cultural and textual analysis. As I wrote this book, a striking succession of events transpired in public culture that dramatized the very problematic with which I have been principally concerned: the inexorable connections among and between constructions of race, class, gender, and sexuality. Controversies surrounding the Clarence Thomas Supreme Court nomination and Senate confirmation hearings, the Mike Tyson rape trial, the O. J. Simpson criminal and civil trials, the Susan Smith murder trial, the Sgt.

Major McKinney sexual misconduct trial, and the passage of anti-immigrant and anti-affirmative action voter initiatives (to name but a few) all made evident both the complex histories of race and gender positionalities in the United States and shifts in ideas of citizenship and civil rights. Key players in most of these incidents self-consciously manipulated race and gender ideologies, forcing even the mainstream media to begin to examine widely-held assumptions about American identities. The debates concerning these spectacles and changes in social policy thus required analyses that explore how race, gender, class, and sexuality constitute each other and disrupt convenient essentialisms.

To take but one example, let us consider the uproar surrounding the nomination of Clarence Thomas to the Supreme Court. Anyone who still believed in the existence of a monolithic black community in 1991 would have had that faith shaken by the responses his nomination provoked. For the nomination and Senate confirmation hearings provided an early and highly visible instance of the uses to which the politics of racial essentialism might be put within a cynical conservative agenda. Changes in the meanings of race and class that emerged out of the expansion of the black middle and underclasses in the "post-Civil Rights era" had clearly made it easier for white conservatives to nominate African Americans who would deny the historical significance of policies such as affirmative action and desegregation, endorse and implement legislation and initiatives hostile to the interests of minorities and the poor and, most importantly, shield them from accusations of racism. By putting Thomas's name forward, George Bush intended to challenge charges that his appointees and policies were harmful to minority concerns. He and his party could hardly be accused of racism if he nominated the second African American to a seat on the Supreme Court. Conversely, he hoped to silence opposition by creating a situation in which no one could object to Thomas's opinions without being called a racist.

Thomas's nomination opened up widespread debates about the various meanings and expectations that attach to the idea of the "African-American appointment" and illuminated significant differences within a black community that has expected (and been expected by others) to offer monolithic support to black candidates and nominees. In a system in which blacks typically have been grossly underrepresented, the advancement of even one has often been read as a step forward for all. But Thomas's relative inexperience and record of hostility to the Civil Rights agenda and the reforms of the Great Society made race alone an insufficient basis for many black moderates and progressives (as well as those of other races) to endorse his candidacy. And of course, Anita Hill's testimony further complicated "black opinion." On the one hand, it confirmed his unsuitability for an appointment to the Court as far as feminists (women and men alike) were concerned. But on the other hand, it consolidated neo-nationalist support among a constituency that had previously condemned Thomas's opportunistic efforts to "transcend" race and undermine the very policies from which he had benefitted.[1] Shored up by anti-feminism that masked itself as racial solidarity, the latter group was willing to ignore their ideological differences with Thomas, rally around him as a black man they perceived to be a victim, and discredit the black woman who accused him of sexual harassment. But the former group envisioned a successor to Justice Marshall who possessed his commitment to justice and social change, not merely someone who belonged to the same racial group.

The significance of this event and others was intensified by their spectacularization within mass media. The seemingly endless succession of these episodes, and the codes by which they have been narrativized and made visible, prompted scholars from a range of fields to undertake cultural analyses that counteract the work of television news. The Thomas hearings, the shooting of Latasha Harlins, the beating of Rodney King, the 1992 Los Angeles uprising, and the Simpson car chase and criminal trial, were all played out and endlessly circulated in visual media. To borrow Robert Gooding-Williams's formulation, if television news "tends to obscure the quotidian setting of [an] event's occurrence," many of the ideologically-based analyses of newsworthy events have sought to acknowledge from cultural, sociological, economic, legal, historical, and/or feminist perspectives, "the complicated ways in which [they] develop out of the situations which engender them."[2] Moreover, this work has challenged disciplinary boundaries and undermined the much-touted divide between the academy and the world outside.[3]

While these controversies have prompted many critics and teachers to challenge putative separations between theory and practice, or between universities and their communities, our classrooms are the places where those oppositions are contested most consistently. We often speak as if teaching and scholarship are separable commitments, but most of us acknowledge that teaching and research inform and transform each other. The links between these enterprises became abundantly clear to me on the day when I attempted to teach a film that explores the impact of urban crisis on constructions of class, gender, and race while my own city was on the verge of erupting around me. That day, my classroom became a space where theoretical explorations met lived realities; the relationships between my students and me and among my students became the sites where we negotiated a redefinition of our identities.

In this concluding chapter I read Haile Gerima's *Bush Mama* (the film I was slated to teach on April 29, 1992) against the backdrop of the Los Angeles uprising that began that day in the wake of the acquittal of the officers who beat Rodney King. I explore here how a "real life" event shaped the discussion of a cinematic text, revealing tensions and contradictions within race, gender, and class identities. At a moment when the artificially constructed boundaries between neighborhoods and racial and ethnic groups were threatened, the boundaries that previously had constructed the social space of the classroom were likewise under scrutiny. We were forced to acknowledge the inseparability of both the text and the classroom from the world outside.

During the spring of 1992 I taught a senior seminar on African-American film at UCLA for the first time. Besides offering a historical survey of the genre, I used black feminist theories of intersectionality to explore with my students how ideologies of gender and race inflect the search for an authentic black subject and a culturally specific cinematic practice throughout the history of U.S. black cinema. We discussed how early African-American films such as The Colored Players' *Scar of Shame*, Oscar Micheaux's *God's Stepchildren*, and Spencer Williams's *Go Down, Death!*, all of which centered on upright, middle-class characters, performed the work of racial uplift by punishing immorality and revising popular stereotypes of black buffoons and reprobates. By mid-April, we had considered how blaxploitation films of the early to mid-seventies responded to the bourgeois propriety of early black independent films and of mainstream race problem movies with their focus on black and white criminality and the urban black working poor, constructing these subjects and types as more racially authentic than members of the black middle class. On April 29, we were scheduled to discuss Haile Gerima's *Bush Mama*.

Set likewise in the urban context, specifically Los Angeles, *Bush Mama* is also concerned with how black representations can subvert conventional stereotypes. However, Gerima's critique extends much further than do those of the studio-financed blaxploitation pictures that preceded his film. As is customary with experimental and oppositional filmmakers, here and in his other works Gerima disrupts defining techniques of mainstream cinema such as continuity editing and narrative linearity to problematize the familiar relationship between viewer and film and to call attention to the artificiality of the medium. His experiments are always challenging and rigorous productions. Nevertheless, his evident conviction that stylistic and thematic change brings us closer to the narratives of real black people returns us to the problematic quest for the authentic black subject.

In an essay on his own cinematic practice and process that focuses on his 1982 film *Ashes and Embers*, Gerima describes the link between his aesthetic choices and the search for authenticity:

> Whenever we have the opportunity to create using the powerful, exorbitantly expensive medium of film, we cannot afford to proceed without a concrete, critical understanding of the history of stereotyping of the African race in motion pictures. This historic consciousness should undergird our creative process all the way from concept to idea to the creation of characters, and on to the further development of the characters' relationships to each other on the vast canvas of the screen plot.[4]

Having acknowledged that his cinematic practice is constructed in opposition to popular representations of black people, he writes elsewhere in the same essay that:

> Blacks have been victimized and corrupted by the conventions of motion pictures and literature, which have removed multidimensional emotional and intellectual depth from our lives ....
>
> We can never transmit our repressed and untold stories by using the very conventions that have devastated us. More specifically, filmmakers, audiences, and critics

must carefully scrutinize and, if necessary, change the traditional screen-audience relationship. The initial step involves our consciously rejecting the falsely imposed aesthetics that have dominated, and still dominate, film terminologies....

We have to democratize the screen, struggle to insure that agents of all looks be represented.[5]

With these statements, Gerima acknowledges his faith in the power of the medium to enact social change, and to express the complexities of human life, in this instance black life in particular. Moreover, he suggests that the conventions of classic Hollywood cinema are complicit with the racist ideology that undergirds stereotypical representations; only by subverting those conventions and reconstructing the position of the spectator can cinema begin to perform an oppositional function.

In the period leading up to the making of *Bush Mama*, Gerima was a leading figure in the group of UCLA-based and -trained black filmmakers that critic Clyde Taylor has called the L. A. Rebellion. He includes under that appellation directors such as Charles Burnett, Billy Woodberry, Larry Clark and later, Julie Dash, Alile Sharon Larkin, and Monona Wali, although some of the filmmakers have expressed some resistance to Taylor's categorization. Taylor has written that although the films made by "Rebellion" directors reflect an extraordinary degree of stylistic and thematic diversity, they share certain features. He thus confirms Gerima's statements when he writes:

[These directors] project onto a social space ... rather than the privatistic, individualistic space of Hollywood's film theater.... It is a space carrying a commitment, in echoes and connotations, to the particular social experience of Afro-American people. It establishes only the slightest, if any, departure from the contiguous, offscreen reality.[6]

To the extent that directors such as Gerima situated their characters in a "social space," they rejected the bourgeois individualist ethos inscribed within mainstream cinematic practice. Gerima and his colleagues drew inspiration from the work of Italian Neo-realist directors such as Roberto Rossellini, Luchino Visconti, and Vittorio De Sica, who sought ways to visually represent characters in socio-political context and who were committed ideologically to bringing to screen narratives of the lives of those whom mainstream cinematic practice had typically ignored.

As Taylor remarks, Gerima and his colleagues "treat space poetically, following the co-ordinates of a propulsive social idea."[7] This description accurately captures the project of *Bush Mama*, for the film attempts to place the narrative of the central character in the context of an analysis of state and international oppression.[8] The film centers on Dorothy, a black, single mother struggling to raise her daughter, Luann, on welfare in Los Angeles. Dorothy is besieged by virtually every difficulty to which a woman in her circumstances might be vulnerable: from time to time she seems to have a drinking problem; her partner, T. C., is in jail, having been falsely accused of an unspecified crime; she can't find work; social services tries to force her to abort the child she is carrying; and before the film ends, she has killed a police officer whom she catches in the act of raping her daughter.

While *Bush Mama* is explicitly about the struggles that Dorothy and others in her community wage against an oppressive state apparatus, it is also a film about education. When we first meet Dorothy, she is in a state of denial, drowning her sorrows in alcohol. Material comforts are her only goals. And she is prone to shut out the voices of other people. When T. C. or her friend Molly try to share their hopes with her, or share some secret from their past, she repeats, even in jest, "Stop T. C., you lyin'," or "Stop Molly, you lyin'."

Throughout the course of the film, Dorothy is educated indirectly in two ways. First, she learns from T. C. to place her own circumstances in historical context. As he reads the history of African-American oppression and resistance, he shares his knowledge with her in his letters from prison. And secondly, as she hears and overhears the "lectures" her young neighbor Angie delivers about the connections between capitalism and racism at home and colonialism abroad, she comes to see her condition as part of a broader diasporic situation. As the film progresses, then, Dorothy comes to desire more than mere alcohol and creature comforts; she grows increasingly aware of the fact that her condition is the result of global inequities in the distribution of power and resources.

Gerima does more than use the medium to show Dorothy's education; through his critique of realist cinematic practice, he makes his viewers increasingly self-conscious about the process of watching film. He uses flashback, and especially the multi-layered voicetrack, to create the illusion of simultaneity so that we see how the military-industrial complex, law enforcement, and social services conspire to police the lives of urban black people, and how capitalism and commodified Christianity function interdependently. Indeed, at several points in the film, it is impossible to distinguish background from foregrounded sound. This confusion challenges the hierarchy upon which Hollywood cinema rests, by which individuals are extracted from their social circumstances and the urban underclass typically is relegated to the margins of the text. In *Bush Mama*, in contrast, the poor are the foreground, and context is as significant as text.

In the opening sequence, Gerima begins his redefinition of the cinematic process. The multilayered voicetrack, on which the repeated questions of a social services employee compete with the voice of the police dispatcher, draws the analogy between different modes by which the urban underclass is policed.

▲ ▲ ▲ ▲ ▲

Moreover, the camera deliberately refuses to relegate Dorothy to the sexualized space that women in front of the camera all too often occupy. When it follows her walking the streets of Los Angeles, it holds the tight close up on her feet and ankles, or on part of her hip, but refuses to pull back to the familiar medium or long shot that would address a spectator constructed as male. Perhaps most strikingly, the slow motion opening sequence challenges the notion of an autonomous, circumscribed cinematic product, for this sequence is actual footage of two members of the crew of *Bush Mama* being harassed by LAPD. The use of this footage as a prologue for a film about the policing of black people's lives projects the film into the social space that surrounds it, as both Taylor and Teshome Gabriel have noted.

From Dorothy's reflection at the end of the film, we may deduce that the narrative contained here is a series of flashbacks on the events that lead up to the murder she commits and her incarceration. Throughout the film, however, it is never entirely clear when we are witnessing the past, when the narrative present, when dream, when reality. This narrative indeterminacy reveals the extent to which Dorothy's destiny is predetermined by myriad forces and demonstrates as well the nightmare quality of her lived experience.

My students, who had viewed *Bush Mama* on Monday, June 27, found Gerima's intentions and achievements beside the point. They were quick to criticize the film, complaining that they considered it to be "depressing and too slow." They wanted a particular level of entertainment, better production values, and a more upbeat, or at least more empowering narrative. Moreover, they resisted the idea that a radical critique of the state apparatus might require an interrogation of conventional Hollywood cinematic practice.

But their responses were profoundly shaped by the discussion that ensued two days later. Our analysis of the film was

▲ ▲ ▲ ▲ ▲

overshadowed by the fact that the verdicts in the trial of the officers who beat Rodney King were scheduled to be announced during our regular class period. Midway through the seminar, someone turned on a radio. We sat in stunned silence as one officer after another was declared "not guilty."[9] Not surprisingly, the verdicts shaped our lives in myriad ways over the course of subsequent weeks and months. But the striking convergence of cinematic text and cultural crisis also affected our understanding of the film and our interaction as a group in ways that I could not have anticipated.

For example, when we met next, several students felt the need, without my prompting, to revise their initial responses to Gerima's work. Not only did the verdict and subsequent uprising force them to consider the extent to which their lives were regulated by law enforcement and the media, but these events also emphasized for them the power of representational practices to undergird and sustain the manipulative power of the state. While the impact of the film was initially lost on most of them, when juxtaposed with media coverage of the uprising and, especially, the defense attorneys' and Simi Valley jurors' interpretations of the videotape of the King beating, they began to appreciate the prescience of Gerima's film. The uses to which so-called documentary evidence had been put in these incidents and others underscored the profound implication of visual culture in the construction and reproduction of racialized, social subjects.

Like most African Americans and progressives of other racial and ethnic groups, they recognized that the verdicts were the real flashpoint in the sequence of events that began with the beating; the horror of the beating notwithstanding, cases of police brutality are sufficiently frequent that they cease to surprise us in and of themselves.[10] The fact that the King beating was captured on video promised to provide incontrovertible evidence, if not a guarantee, that at least this misuse of police authority would not go unpunished. But the change of venue to predominantly Anglo Simi Valley set the stage for the verdicts' inexorable connection to white flight and racism. The verdicts themselves spoke volumes about the persistence of injustice and the depths of racism in this country. Moreover, they wounded so many so deeply for they revealed just how profoundly even the most cynical of us believe in the defining power of the visual image.[11] As Judith Butler has so aptly argued, the reversal of the video's evident "meaning" exposed the extent to which ideologies of race and domination structure the domain of the visible:

> ...when the visual is fully schematized by racism, the "visual evidence" to which one refers will always and only refute the conclusions based upon it; for it is possible within this racist episteme that no black person can seek recourse to the visible as the sureground of evidence....The visual field is not neutral to the question of race; it is itself a racial formation, an episteme, hegemonic and forceful.[12]

When the video was first released, its meaning seemed incontestable; most viewers readily acknowledged that King had been restrained by means of excessive force. But by breaking the eighty-one-second video down into a series of still images, the defense attorneys were able to use it to support a counternarrative that constructed King as the threat and the brutality of the police officers as self-defense.[13] This radical reinterpretation dramatized the extent to which the body of the black male is always already coded as dangerous; it eerily revoiced Gerima's cinematic and discursive exploration of the relationship between image and ideology. For my students, then, the notion that film might project itself into "social space" acquired particular force once *Bush Mama* was "read" in relation to this sequence of contemporaneous events.

Media coverage of the trial and verdicts thus highlighted the overdetermined nature of racialized visual representations. It also intensified the general awareness of race, class, ethnicity, and the distribution of power in late twentieth-century America, illuminating differences within communities that melting pot rhetoric and convenient group labels often obscured.[14] It challenged us to think more deeply about the meaning of race and ethnicity when "white" is neither the normative category nor the inevitable "other."

Televised accounts of the uprising characterized Angelenos by race and ethnicity: victimized Korean shopkeepers fought off marauding black and Latino looters and "rioters" who destroyed their own communities in "South Central" and much of Koreatown. Anglos on the west side, and in the surrounding valley and coastal communities commented on the uprising, and looked on in fear and horror, but were generally sheltered from the violence. The media thus imposed upon the city a spatially arranged racial and cultural narrative that entrapped even those of us who struggled to maintain critical distance from it. For weeks strangers, colleagues, and acquaintances viewed each other with suspicion, finding it difficult to separate ourselves and each other from these positions. Returning to class two days after the verdicts and uprising, I was forced to confront some of the complexities of a multi-racial classroom at a moment of cultural crisis. More than at any other time before or since then, I understood something of the difference race and gender make in the classroom. The students in this course represented a diverse cross-section of UCLA undergraduates. Over half were African American; the rest were Asian American, Latino/a, and white. Demographics notwithstanding, we shared a tacit understanding that race, gender, sexuality, and ethnicity were speakable as categories of textual analysis, and sometimes even speakable as categories of personal experience, when those experiences enhanced the analysis of a film or reading. As I realized only in retrospect, I had prided myself on sustaining an atmosphere in which social and intellectual differences were acknowledged, but no single position enjoyed special privileges.[15] But in the classroom as in the city, the verdicts and the uprising revealed the deep divides barely concealed by the fiction of color neutrality; the events affected my students differently and they claimed those experiences in different ways.

Because we had heard the verdicts for the first time together, because the course dealt with issues of race and representation, and because we could not possibly have avoided it, we began the next class meeting by talking about the uprising and the media coverage. Many of the African-American students wondered how they could justify sitting in a classroom at a moment that called for visible acts of resistance. More than a few identified with King's victimization at the hands of the police. An Asian-American and a Latina student both articulated a position of solidarity with the African-American struggle against a racist law enforcement and judiciary system. Most of the white students said nothing, but one white male student was concerned that African Americans would identify him with the jurors and assume that he was a racist.

The white student spoke with greater persistence than any of the other students did. And at first, I allowed him to lament his situation. But as the African-American students began to direct their energies toward reassuring him, I could not help but intervene. I could not let him continue to demand attention, and I could not let the others continue to provide it, without at least commenting on the implications of the fact that he had centered his own position at the expense of their own. At that moment, I realized that race and gender identities had assumed new significance; as the boundary between text and context had blurred, so the social meanings of our identities had bled into our well-defined classroom roles.

On that day and during the days that followed, as I negotiated a multiplicity of public and private roles, textual analysis seemed to provide the only safe and familiar space. For indeed, every aspect of the Rodney King episode, from the beating to the uprising, offered possibilities for critique. Every chapter in the sequence of events seemed to engage questions of gender, race, sexuality, class, representation, ethnicity, geography, and community, to the point that each exchange, every image, was a text to be scrutinized. Examining the classroom dynamics in the context of the uprising became yet another way to consider how the disturbances had affected our lives, another way to understand the various ways in which our identities are constituted.

Cheryl Harris has written that the idea of colorblindness protects the property interest in whiteness: "As Neil Gotanda has argued, colorblindness is a form of race subordination in that it denies the historical context of white domination and Black subordination. This idea of race recasts privileges attendant to whiteness as legitimate race identity under 'neutral' colorblind principles."[16] Even as the disingenuous use of the notion of colorblindness has been used to justify practices that exclude those who have historically suffered disenfranchisement, intersectionality can provide a valuable way of ensuring that race and gender remain visible and speakable in all their multiplicity. Acknowledging the multifarious ways in which race and gender are constructed gives the lie to the notion that identities are mere accidents of birth. Events that transpired in the aftermath of the King beating begin to suggest how intersectionality as a mode of reading can function to illuminate not only connections between gender, race, and sexuality, but also those between fact and fiction, text and "real life," classroom and outside world, and private and public identities. For just as the primary categories of analysis are mutually constitutive constructions, so the linking of film, class, and urban crisis here points to the inseparability of representational and pedagogical practices from the culture in which we live.

▲ ▲ ▲ ▲ ▲

NOTES TO THE PREFACE

1. Nell Irvin Painter has challenged the authenticity of the most popular version of Sojourner Truth's 1851 Akron, Ohio speech (commonly termed the "Ain't [or Ar'n't] I A Woman" speech). See her "Representing Truth: Sojourner Truth's Knowing and Becoming Known," *Journal of American History* 81, no. 2 (September 1994): 461–92 and *Sojourner Truth: A Life, A Symbol* (New York: W. W. Norton, 1996). See also Cheryl I. Harris's insightful analysis of various accounts of the 1851 speech in "Finding Sojourner's Truth: Race, Gender and the Institution of Property," *Cardozo Law Review* 18 (November 1996): 309–409.

2. See Kimberlé W. Crenshaw, "Demarginalizing the Intersection of Race and Sex: A Black Feminist Critique of Antidiscrimination Doctrine, Feminist Theory and Antiracist Politics," *The University of Chicago Legal Forum* (1989): 139–67.

3. Although I take issue with some of the presuppositions of his larger argument, I do share Orlando Patterson's sense that questions around the construction of masculinity fall within the province of black feminism. See "Blacklash: The Crisis of Gender Relations Among African Americans," *Transition* 62 (Summer 1994): 4–26. For a sustained exploration of the impact of race, sexuality, and class upon constructions of masculinity, see *Representing Black Men,* ed. Marcellus Blount and George P. Cunningham (New York: Routledge, 1996).

4. Mari Matsuda describes this process in the following manner: "The way I try to understand the interconnection of all forms of subordination is through a method I call 'ask the other question.' When I see something that looks racist, I ask, 'Where is the patriarchy in this?' When I see something that looks sexist, I ask, 'Where is the heterosexism in this?' When I see something that looks homophobic, I ask, 'Where are the class interests in this?'" See Mari J. Matsuda, "Beside My Sister, Facing the Enemy: Legal Theory Out of Coalition," *Stanford Law Review* 43 (July 1991): 1189.

5. For an insightful discussion of this debate, see Margaret Homans, "'Racial Composition:' Metaphor and the Body in the Writing of Race," in *Female Subjects in Black and White: Race, Psychoanalysis,*

NOTES TO THE PREFACE

Feminism, ed., Elizabeth Abel, Barbara Christian, and Helene Moglen (Berkeley and Los Angeles: University of California Press, 1997), pp. 77–101.

6. Valerie Smith, "Black Feminist Theory and the Representation of the 'Other,'" in *Changing Our Own Words: Essays on Criticism, Theory, and Writing by Black Women,* ed., Cheryl A. Wall (New Brunswick, NJ: Rutgers University Press, 1989), p. 39.

7. Barbara Smith, "Toward a Black Feminist Criticism," *Conditions: Two* 1, no. 2 (October 1977), reprinted in *But Some of Us Are Brave: Black Women's Studies,* ed., Gloria T. Hull, Patricia Bell Scott, and Barbara Smith, (1982), pp. 157–75.

8. Patricia Hill Collins, *Black Feminist Thought: Knowledge, Consciousness, and the Politics of Empowerment* (Boston: Unwin Hyman, 1990).

9. See Hazel Carby, *Reconstructing Womanhood: The Emergence of the Afro-American Woman Novelist* (New York: Oxford University Press, 1987), p. 10, and Ann duCille, *The Coupling Convention: Sex, Text, and Tradition in Black Women's Fiction* (New York: Oxford University Press, 1993), pp. 6–7.

10. Stuart Hall, "What is this 'Black' in *Black Popular Culture?*" in *Black Popular Culture,* ed., Gina Dent, (Seattle: Bay Press, 1992), p. 31.

11. Joan W. Scott, "The Evidence of Experience," *Critical Inquiry* 17 (Summer 1991): 778.

12. Stuart Hall, "Cultural Identity and Cinematic Representation," in *Ex-Iles: Essays on Caribbean Cinema,* ed., Mbye B. Cham, (Trenton, NJ: Africa World Press, 1992), p. 220.

13. I am indebted here to the work of scholars who have been willing to negotiate the ostensibly self-contradictory space between identities understood to be discursively constructed and social relations enacted

by and upon real people. See Gayatri Chakravorty Spivak, "Strategy, Identity, Writing" (1986), rpt. in *The Post-Colonial Critic: Interviews, Strategies, Dialogues,* ed., Sarah Harasym, (New York: Routledge, 1990), pp. 35–49; Linda Alcoff, "Cultural Feminism Versus Post-Structuralism: The Identity Crisis in Feminist Theory," *Signs* 13, no. 3 (1988): pp. 405–36; and David Van Leer, *The Queening of America: Gay Culture in Straight Society* (New York: Routledge, 1995). This tension also lies at the heart of Marlon Riggs's posthumously released film, *Black Is...Black Ain't* (1996).

14. See Deborah McDowell's insightful analysis of the status of black feminism and theory in the academy generally and in feminist discourses more specifically in *"The Changing Same": Black Women's Literature, Criticism, and Theory* (Bloomington: Indiana University Press, 1995), pp. 156–75.

15. See *Theorizing Black Feminisms: The Visionary Pragmatism of Black Women,* ed. Stanlie M. James and Abena P. A. Busia (London and New York: Routledge, 1993).

16. McDowell, *"The Changing Same,"* p. 160.

17. Valerie Smith, "Split Affinities: The Case of Interracial Rape," in *Conflicts in Feminism,* ed. Marianne Hirsch and Evelyn Fox Keller (New York: Routledge, 1990), pp. 271–87.

18. For Gloria Anzaldúa, the borderland is "a vague and undetermined place created by the emotional residue of an unnatural boundary," an area "in a constant state of transition." See her *Borderlands/La Frontera: The New Mestiza* (San Francisco: Spinsters/Aunt Lute, 1987). For two brilliant discussions of the significance of this text, see Yvonne Yarbro-Bejarano, "Gloria Anzaldúa's *Borderlands/La Frontera:* Cultural Studies, 'Difference,' and the Non-Unitary Subject," *Cultural Studies* (Fall 1994): 5–28, and Sonia Saldívar-Hull, *Feminism on the Border: Contemporary Chicana Writers* (Berkeley and Los Angeles: University of California Press, 1998).

For Mary Poovey, border cases are "sites of intensive debates...[that

NOTES TO THE PREFACE

threaten] to challenge [the construction of sexual difference] *the opposition* upon which all other oppositions are claimed to be based." See her *Unveven Developments: The Ideological Work of Gender in Mid-Victorian England* (Chicago: University of Chicago Press, 1988), p. 12.

19. Cheryl I. Harris, "Myths of Race and Gender in the Trials of O. J. Simpson and Susan Smith—Spectacles of Our Times," *Washburn Law Journal* 35, no. 2 (1996): 231. Elsewhere, drawing on the work of Angela Davis, bell hooks, Elizabeth V. Spelman, and Kimberlé Williams Crenshaw, Harris defines racial patriarchy in the following manner: "Racial patriarchy describes that social, political, economic, legal and conceptual system that entrenched the ideology of white supremacy and white male control over women's reproduction and sexuality. This system operated by subordinating all Black people along lines that were articulated within and through gender, and all women along lines that were articulated within and through race." See "Finding Sojourner's Truth," p. 312.

NOTES TO CHAPTER ONE

1. See Angela Y. Davis, "Rape, Racism and the Myth of the Black Rapist," in *Women, Race and Class* (New York: Random House, 1983), pp. 172–201.

2. Jacquelyn Dowd Hall, "'The Mind That Burns in Each Body': Women, Rape, and Racial Violence," in *Powers of Desire: The Politics of Sexuality,* ed., Ann Snitow, Christine Stansell, and Sharon Thompson (New York: Monthly Review Press), pp. 329–49.

3. As George P. Cunningham argues, "[These] acts that intertwine power, violence, and sexuality—ultimately reduced to figures of various violated bodies—emerged into national consciousness as public spectacles and codes for the nature and well being of the body politic." (134–35) For a compelling article that reads a series of recent cases in relation to the lynching of Emmett Till, in "Body Politics: Race, Gender, and the Captive Body," in *Representing Black Men,* pp. 131–54.

A series of important and influential cultural studies texts on these public spectacles have appeared, including: Toni Morrison, ed., *Racing Justice, En-gendering Power: Essays on Anita Hill, Clarence Thomas, and the Construction of Social Reality* (New York: Pantheon, 1992); Robert Gooding-Williams, ed., *Reading Rodney King, Reading Urban Uprising* (New York: Routledge, 1993); Toni Morrison and Claudia Brodsky Lacour, ed., *Birth of a Nation'hood: Gaze, Script, and Spectacle in the O. J. Simpson Case* (New York: Pantheon, 1997); and Darnell M. Hunt, *Screening the Los Angeles "Riots:" Race, Seeing, and Resistance* (New York: Cambridge University Press, 1997).

4. This chapter expands the argument of my earlier essay, "Split Affinities: the Case of Interracial Rape," in *Conflicts in Feminism,* ed. Marianne G. Hirsch and Evelyn Fox Keller (New York; Routledge, Chapman and Hall, 1990), pp. 271–87. For this version I explore two key issues that received insufficient attention in the earlier piece: the perspective of the so-called "black press" on incidents of interracial rape and the black feminist response to such cases.

My argument is greatly indebted to Cheryl I. Harris's article about the nature of the O. J. Simpson criminal trial and the Susan Smith trial. See "Myths of Race and Gender in the Trials of O. J. Simpson and Susan Smith—Spectacles of Our Times," *Washburn Law Journal* 35.2 (1996): 225–53. I have found especially useful her observation that in the context of these high-profile cases, there are two trials: "one is situated in the courthouse, and the other in the public arena, where much more is at stake than the individual guilt or innocence of the defendant. In the public trial, while determination of ultimate responsibility is important, it is the publicly inscribed image and meaning—the representations that are constructed—that are of equal, if not greater, significance." (227)

5. Ida B. Wells, *Crusade for Justice: The Autobiography of Ida B. Wells* (Chicago: University of Chicago Press, 1970), p. 64.

6. Stephanie H. Jed discusses the relationship between the rape of Lucretia and the creation of republican Rome in *Chaste Thinking: The Rape of Lucretia and the Birth of Humanism* (Bloomington: Indiana University Press, 1989). See also Norman Bryson, "Two Narratives of Rape in the Visual Arts: Literature and the Visual Arts," in *Rape: An Historical and Social Enquiry,* ed., Sylvana Tomaselli and Roy Porter (New York: Basil Blackwell, 1986), pp. 152–73.

7. Jennifer Wriggins, "Rape, Racism, and the Law," *Harvard Women's Law Journal* 6 (1983), 105–06.

8. For a systematic analysis of the ways in which Susan Brownmiller and some other early feminist discussions of rape use the figure of the black male rapist see Angela Y. Davis, "Rape, Racism and the Myth of the Black Rapist," pp. 178–82.

9. See Susan Estrich, *Real Rape* (Cambridge: Harvard University Press, 1987); Davis, "Rape, Racism and the Myth of the Black Rapist"; and Catherine MacKinnon, "A Rally Against Rape" in *Feminism Unmodified: Discourses on Life and Law* (Cambridge: Harvard University Press, 1987), pp. 81–84.

▲ ▲ ▲ ▲ ▲

NOTES TO CHAPTER ONE

10. MacKinnon, "A Rally Against Rape," p. 81.

11. During the week of the Central Park rape, twenty-eight other first-degree rapes or attempted rapes were reported in New York City. Nearly all the reported rapes involved black women or Latinas. Yet, as Don Terry wrote in the *New York Times,* most went unnoticed by the public. See "A Week of Rapes: The Jogger and 28 Not in the News," the *New York Times,* 5/29/89, p. 25.

12. Andrew Kopkind, "The Stuart Case: Race, Class and Murder in Boston," *The Nation,* February 5, 1990, volume 250, p. 153.

13. For details of the assault and subsequent trials, see Timothy Sullivan, *Unequal Verdicts: The Central Park Jogger Trials* (New York: Simon and Schuster, 1992).

14. It seems to me that the journalistic practice of "protecting the identity" of rape victims needs to be reconsidered. I would argue that leaving victims unnamed objectifies them. Moreover, this silence contributes to the construction of rape as an experience of which the victim ought to be ashamed.

15. Harold L. Jamison, "Another Woman Raped and Strangled to Death," *The Amsterdam News,* May 6, 1989, p. 1.

16. Wilbert A. Tatum, "Koch Must Resign," *The Amsterdam News,* April 29, 1989, p. 1.

17. Jamison, "Leaders Temper Anger with Caution," *The Amsterdam News,* April 29, 1989, p. 3.

18. In the Scottsboro case, nine young black men were tried without benefit of counsel and sentenced to death without substantive evidence that any rape had been committed. Their sentences were eventually commuted and eleven of the defendants released, but only after they had spent a total of 104 years in prison.

19. Grass and semen stains and dirt and debris inside Kevin

▲ ▲ ▲ ▲ ▲

NOTES TO CHAPTER ONE

Richardson's undershorts led to his conviction on charges of attempted murder, rape, sodomy, first degree robbery, three counts of second degree assault, and riot in the first degree. Kharey Wise was convicted of sexual abuse, first degree assault, and riot in the first degree. Steven Lopez, the final defendant, pleaded guilty to the charge of robbing one of the four men who was also attacked in the park on the night of the rape, and received a sentence of one and one half to four and one half years in a state youth correctional center.

20. I have found useful here Patricia Hill Collins's use of the term "the outsider-within" to characterize the black feminist perspective. See *Black Feminist Thought,* pp. 11–13.

21. Jennifer Wriggins makes this point as well. See "Rape and Racism," p. 140.

22. I am grateful to Mary Helen Washington for calling my attention to Reginald McKnight's "Quitting Smoking," another complex representation of the vexed issues that surround the telling of interracial rape. The story appears in his collection, *The Kind of Light That Shines On Texas* (Boston: Little, Brown and Company, 1992), pp. 139–74.

23. See, for instance, Deborah McDowell's discussion of Walker's "Source," in her essay "Reading Family Matters" in *Changing Our Own Words: Essays on Criticism, Theory, and Writing by Black Women,* ed., Cheryl A. Wall (New Brunswick, NJ: Rutgers University Press, 1989), pp. 75–97.

24. Barbara Christian, "The Race for Theory," in *Gender and Theory: Dialogues on Feminist Criticism,* ed., Linda Kauffman (New York: Basil Blackwell, 1989), p. 226.

25. Alice Walker, "Advancing Luna—and Ida B. Wells," in *You Can't Keep A Good Woman Down* (New York: Harcourt Brace Jovanovich, 1981), p. 85. Subsequent references will be to this edition and will be noted in the text by page number.

▲▼▲▼▲▼

NOTES TO CHAPTER ONE

26. I problematize the figure of the author here to make clear that I do not intend to refer to Alice Walker, but rather to the multiplicity of narrative selves that is generated out of the disintegrating of the text.

27. This need not always be the case. See Mary Helen Washington's discussion of teaching this story in her essay "How Racial Differences Helped Us Discover Our Common Ground," in *Gendered Subjects: The Dynamics of Feminist Teaching,* eds. Margo Culley and Catherine Portuges (Boston: Routledge, Kegan Paul, 1985), pp. 221–29.

28. Given the rise of problematic uses of the notion of a color-blind society, and the frequency of observations that the Rodney King beating, the O. J. Simpson trial, and the rise of anti-affirmative action legislation are not about race, this comment now seems less surprising, more a harbinger of things to come.

29. Teresa de Lauretis, "Feminist Studies/Critical Studies: Issues, Terms, and Contexts," in *Feminist Studies/Critical Studies,* ed., de Lauretis (Bloomington: Indiana University Press, 1986), p. 14.

NOTES TO CHAPTER TWO

1. The idea of the "passing plot" encompasses many different kinds of stories. I use the term to refer to narratives that focus on the consequences of being genotypically black for a character or characters who pass for white, at least intermittently. I have in mind novels and films such as: William Dean Howells's *An Imperative Duty* (1891), Mark Twain's *Pudd'nhead Wilson* (1894), Charles W. Chesnutt's *The House Behind the Cedars* (1890), James Weldon Johnson's *The Autobiography of an Ex-Colored Man* (1912), Jessie Fauset's *Plum Bun* (1928), Nella Larsen's *Passing* (1929), Fannie Hurst's *Imitation of Life* (1933), Oscar Micheaux's *God's Stepchildren* (1937), Willard Savoy's *Alien Land,* Alfred L. Werker's *Lost Boundaries*, and Elia Kazan's *Pinky* (all 1949).

2. Several insightful essays on the interconnections of race and gender in passing plots have informed my work here, although they focus primarily on written narratives. See especially Barbara Christian, *Black Women Novelists: The Development of a Tradition, 1892–1976* (Westport, CT: Greenwood Press, 1980), pp. 35–61; Cheryl A. Wall, "Passing for What?: Aspects of Identity in Nella Larsen's Novels," *Black American Literature Forum* 20 (1986): 97–111; Deborah E. McDowell, "Introduction" in Nella Larsen, *"Quicksand" and "Passing"* (New York: Knopf, 1929; rpt. New Brunswick, NJ: Rutgers University Press, 1986), pp. ix–xxxvii; and David Van Leer, *The Queening of America: Gay Culture in Straight Society* (New York: Routledge, 1995).

3. I draw here on Manthia Diawara's theory of a resistant black spectator that revises earlier work by Christian Metz, Laura Mulvey, and Stephen Heath, and on bell hooks's essay on black feminist spectatorship. See Diawara, "Black Spectatorship: Problems of Identification and Resistance," *Screen* 29 (Winter 1988): pp. 66–76, and hooks, "The Oppositional Gaze: Black Female Spectators," in *Black Looks: Race and Representation* (Boston: South End Press, 1992), pp. 115–31.

4. Jessie Redmon Fauset, *Plum Bun: A Novel Without a Moral* (New York: Frederick A. Stokes, 1928; rpt. New York: Pandora Press, 1985), 69.

▲ ▲ ▲ ▲ ▲

NOTES TO CHAPTER TWO

5. Consider, for instance, Charles Chesnutt's John Walden Warwick, James Weldon Johnson's unnamed protagonist, or Willard Savoy's Kern Roberts.

6. I have in mind here Hurst's and Stahl's Peola, Sirk's Sarah Jane, and Larsen's Clare Kendry, for example.

7. My survey of the literature on *Imitation of Life* shows that more critical attention has been directed to the 1959 remake. Lucy Fischer has written that the 1959 *Imitation* has been the subject of much recent attention because of a heightened interest in French auteurist theory and the emergence of genre studies and an increased attention to melodrama. Moreover, as she writes, "Imitation also profited from the currency of ideological criticism. Its inclusion of dominant black characters in a period of heightened racial awareness attracted writers concerned with color and class. Its status as a 'woman's picture' (focusing on the struggles of two single working mothers) made it ripe for feminist investigation." See "Three-Way Mirror: *Imitation of Life*" in *Imitation of Life*, ed. Lucy Fischer (New Brunswick, NJ: Rutgers University Press, 1991), p. 5.

8. Judith Butler, "Lana's 'Imitation': Melodramatic Repetition and the Gender Performative," *Genders* 9 (Fall 1990): 1–18; Sandy Flitterman-Lewis, "*Imitation(s) of Life*: The Black Woman's Double Determination as Troubling 'Other,'" in Fischer, *Imitation of Life*, pp. 325–35; and Lauren Berlant, "National Brands/National Body: *Imitation of Life*" in *Comparative American Identities: Race, Sex, and Nationality in the Modern Text*, ed. Hortense J. Spillers (New York and London: Routledge, 1991), pp. 110–40.

9. For example, see Charles Affron, "Performing Performing: Irony and Affect," *Cinema Journal* 20 (Fall 1980): 42–52; Michael Stern, *Douglas Sirk* (Boston: Twayne, 1979); and Butler, "Lana's 'Imitation.'"

10. Judith Butler's compelling reading of the Sirk remake explores the complexity of "the construction and contestation of the mimetic illusion," but does not critique his constructions of race in terms that exceed those that Sirk establishes.

NOTES TO CHAPTER TWO

11. Toni Morrison, *Playing in the Dark: Whiteness and the Literary Imagination* (Cambridge: Harvard University Press, 1992), pp. 51–52.

12. See Berlant, p. 114.

13. Flitterman-Lewis, pp. 328–29.

14. S. V. Hartman and Farah Jasmine Griffin are not as easily persuaded as I am that Dash submits the passing plot to thorough critique. See their essay, "Are You as Colored as That Negro?: The Politics of Being Seen in Julie Dash's *Illusions,*" *Black American Literature Forum* 25 (Summer 1991): 361–74.

15. See Phyllis Klotman, *Screenplays of the African American Experience* (Bloomington: Indiana University Press, 1991), p. 194.

16. We hear the words of Julius's letter because she reads them in a voiceover. We learn about her mother's opinions indirectly by hearing Mignon's one-sided conversation.

17. Fitzgerald fans will recognize her voice, but the film does not identify the singer until the closing credits.

18. I thank David Van Leer for this observation.

19. The encounter with the racist taxi driver is rapidly becoming a racialized primal scene that marks the "reality" of discrimination; in autobiography, criticism, and film, it signals the moment at which subject and reader/spectator wink at each other in mutual acknowledgment that a middle-class black person (generally male) is still "black," his class position notwithstanding. See, for example, Houston A. Baker, Jr., "Caliban's Triple Play," in *"Race," Writing and Difference,* ed., Henry Louis Gates, Jr. (Chicago: University of Chicago Press, 1986), p. 385; and Cornel West, "Preface," *Race Matters* (Boston: Beacon Press, 1993), p. x. This kind of scene is especially striking in Alan J. Pakula's screen adaptation of John Grisham's *Pelican Brief,* starring Denzel Washington. The race of the male protagonist of the

novel is unidentified and thus he is presumed to be white. On the surface, Pakula's film seems to suggest that a black actor can play this part without substantially changing the story. However, Pakula marks the visibility of Washington's blackness by including a scene in which he is unable to get a taxi and by eliminating the erotic tension between the Washington and the Julia Roberts characters.

20. Hazel Carby, *Reconstructing Womanhood: The Emergence of the Afro-American Woman Novelist* (New York: Oxford University Press, 1987), p. 90.

NOTES TO CHAPTER THREE

1. Glenn C. Loury, "Free At Last? A Personal Perspective on Race and Identity in America," and Reginald McKnight, "Confessions of a Wannabe Negro," in *Lure and Loathing: Essays on Race, Identity, and the Ambivalence of Assimilation,* ed., Gerald Early (New York: Penguin, 1993), pp. 1–12 and 95–112, respectively.

2. E. Franklin Frazier, *The Black Bourgeoisie* (New York: Free Press, 1957; rpt. 1962).

3. Harold Cruse, *The Crisis of the Negro Intellectual* (New York: Quill, 1984), pp. 83–84.

4. Langston Hughes, "The Negro Artist and the Racial Mountain," *The Nation,* June 23, 1926, volume 122, p. 692.

5. Le Roi Jones, "The Myth of a Negro Literature, in *Home, Social Essays* (New York: William Morrow, 1966), p. 110.

6. Jill Nelson, *Volunteer Slavery: My Authentic Negro Experience* (Chicago: Noble Press, 1993); Michele Wallace, *Black Macho and the Myth of the Superwoman* (New York: The Dial Press, 1978; rpt. New York: Verso); Stephen L. Carter, *Reflections of an Affirmative Action Baby* (New York: Basic Books, 1991); and Jake Lamar, B*ourgeois Blues: An American Memoir* (New York: Plume Books, 1992).

7. Thelma Wills Foote, "The Black Intellectual, Recent Curricular Reforms, and the Discourse of Collective Identity," *Radical History Review* 56 (1993): 51–57; Stuart Hall, "Cultural Identity and Cinematic Representation," in *Ex-Iles: Essays on Caribbean Cinema,* ed., Mbye B. Cham (Trenton, NJ: Africa World Press, 1992), pp. 220–36; and Hall, "What is this 'Black' in *Black Popular Culture?*" in *Black Popular Culture,* ed., Gina Dent (Seattle: Bay Press, 1992), pp. 21–33; Wahneema Lubiano, "But Compared to What?: Reading Realism, Representation, and Essentialism in *School Daze, Do the Right Thing,* and the Spike Lee Discourse," *Black American Literature Forum* 25 (Summer 1991): 253–82, rpt. in *Representing Blackness: Issues in Film and Video,* ed., Valerie Smith (New Brunswick: Rutgers

NOTES TO CHAPTER THREE

University Press, 1997) pp. 97–122; Kobena Mercer, "Diaspora Culture and the Dialogic Imagination: The Aesthetics of Black Independent Film in Britain," in *Critical Perspectives on Black Independent Cinema,* ed., Mbye Cham and Claire Andrade-Watkins (Cambridge, MA: MIT Press, 1988), pp. 50–61; Adolph Reed, Jr., "The 'Black Revolution' and the Reconstitution of Blackness," in *Race, Politics and Culture: Critical Essays on the Radicalism of the 1960s* (Greenwood Press, 1986), pp. 61–95; Cornel West, *Race Matters* (Boston: Beacon Press, 1993).

8. Hall, "Black Popular Culture," p. 31.

9. Henry Louis Gates, Jr., "Must Buppiehood Cost Homeboy His Soul?" *New York Times,* Sunday, 1 March 1992, sec. 2.

10. Stuart Hall, "Cultural Identity and Cinematic Representation," p. 220.

11. For a fascinating discussion of *Ricochet* as "an antiaffirmative action parable for the 1990s that is propelled by unfulfilled white male homoerotic desire," (158) see Elizabeth Alexander, "'We're Gonna Deconstruct Your Life!': The Making and un-Making of the Black Bourgeois Patriarch in *Ricochet,*" in *Representing Black Men,* ed., Marcellus Blount and George P. Cunningham (New York: Routledge, 1996), pp. 157–71.

12. Alexander rightly notes the way in which Blake's name underscores the film's anxiety about the economy of power and resources in the affirmative action era: "His name is an English title, but because he is in jail he is a king without a country. His entitlements actually grant him nothing at all, and this rage combusts utterly when a person like Styles—to Blake, all fortune without entitlement—comes along." (160)

NOTES TO CHAPTER FOUR

1. Other work that has problematized the role of "realness" in film and video by people of color includes: Wahneema Lubiano, "But Compared to What?: Reading Realism, Representation, and Essentialism in *School Daze, Do the Right Thing,* and the Spike Lee Discourse," *Black American Literature Forum* 25.2 (Summer 1991): 253–82, rpt. in *Representing Blackness: Issues in Film and Video,* ed., Valerie Smith (New Brunswick: Rutgers University Press, 1997), pp. 97–122; David Van Leer, "Visible Silence: Spectatorship in Black Gay and Lesbian Film," in *Representing Blackness,* pp. 157–81; Stuart Hall, "What is this 'Black' in *Black Popular Culture?*", in *Black Popular Culture,* ed., Gina Dent (Seattle: Bay Press, 1992), pp. 21–33, rpt. in *Representing Blackness,* pp. 123–33; and especially Kobena Mercer, "Diaspora Culture and the Dialogic Imagination: The Aesthetics of Black Independent Film in Britain," *BLACKFRAMES: Critical Perspectives on Black Independent Cinema,* ed. Mbye B. Cham and Claire Andrade-Watkins (Cambridge, MA: MIT Press, 1988), pp. 50–61.

2. This assumption informs such works as Thomas Cripps, *Black Film as Genre* (Bloomington: Indiana University Press, 1978); Ed Guerrero, *Framing Blackness: The African American Image in Film* (Philadelphia: Temple University Press, 1993), and Manthia Diawara, "Black American Cinema: The New Realism" in *Black American Cinema,* ed., Diawara (New York: Routledge, 1993), pp. 3–25.

3. Michael Rogin, "'The Sword Became a Flashing Vision': D. W. Griffith's *The Birth of a Nation,*" in *Ronald Reagan, The Movie, and Other Episodes in Political Demonology* (Berkeley and Los Angeles: University of California Press, 1987), pp. 190–235.

4. Wahneema Lubiano, "But Compared to What?," p. 264.

5. W. J. T. Mitchell, "The Violence of Public Art: *Do the Right Thing,*" *Critical Inquiry* 16 (Summer 1990): 894.

6. Jacquie Jones, "The New Ghetto Aesthetic," *Wide Angle* 13:3–4, 32–43.

7. Bill Nichols, *Representing Reality: Issues and Concepts in Documentary* (Bloomington: Indiana University Press, 1991), pp. ix–x.

8. *Brother to Brother: New Writings by Black Gay Men,* ed., Essex Hemphill (Boston: Alyson Publications, 1991), p. 193.

9. These lines have been published as the poem "Tongues Untied" in *Brother to Brother,* pp. 200–05.

10. For these observations I am indebted to Bill Nichols, *Representing Reality* (Bloomington: Indiana University Press, 1991), pp. 18–32; David Van Leer, "Visible Silence: Spectatorship in Black Gay and Lesbian Film," in *Representing Blackness,* pp. 157–81; and Diana Paulin, "Framing the Truth: Representation and Identities in *Tongues Untied* and *Paris is Burning*" (unpublished manuscript).

11. For insightful critiques of the homophobia of discourses of racial authenticity that consider as well the relationship between black feminism and black gay and lesbian discourses, see Marcellus Blount and George P. Cunningham, "The 'Real' Black Man?" in *Representing Black Men,* ed., Blount and Cunningham (New York: Routledge, 1996), pp. ix–xv; Kendall Thomas, "'Ain't Nothin' Like the Real Thing:' Black Masculinity, Gay Sexuality, and the Jargon of Authenticity," in *Representing Black Men,* pp. 55–69, rpt. in *The House that Race Built: Black Americans, U. S. Terrain,* ed.,Wahneema Lubiano (New York: Pantheon, 1997), pp. 116–35; Rhonda M. Williams, "Living at the Crossroads: Explorations in Race, Nationality, Sexuality, and Gender," in *The House that Race Built,* pp. 136–56; and Alycee Lane, "Homosexuality and the Crisis of Black Particularity," (unpublished dissertation, UCLA, 1997).

12. Thomas, "'Ain't Nothin' Like the Real Thing,'" p. 126.

13. What is clearly missing from this list is black-on-black and gang violence.

14. The song is, of course, taken from the musical based on Lorraine

Hansberry's autobiographical work of the same name. Its use links Riggs's circumstances to Hansberry's, thereby invoking another acclaimed black artist who spoke out against racial, sexual, and gender oppression and died at an early age.

15. In "Visible Silence," David Van Leer suggests that *She Don't Fade* "[appropriates] the title, photography, mock-documentary style, and character asides of Spike Lee's *She's Gotta Have It*." See "Visible Silence," p. 176.

16. Jan Zita Grover, "Dykes in Context: Some Problems in Minority Representation," *The Contest of Meaning: Critical Histories of Photography,* ed. Richard Bolton (Cambridge, MA: The MIT Press, 1993), p. 167.

17. Dunye takes up the issue of the faux documentary in *Watermelon Woman* (1996), her first feature-length film, in which she plays a filmmaker trying to research the life of an imagined black lesbian actor who played mammy figures in Hollywood pictures of the '30s and '40s.

18. Several brief scenes follow Lisa and Kendra, a couple from New York who leave home late, get lost on the way, and arrive at the party at the end of the video.

19. Barbara Lekatsas, "Encounters: The Film Odyssey of Camille Billops," *Black American Literature Forum* 25 (Summer 1991), p. 400.

20. For a deeply suggestive and thoughtful discussion of *Finding Christa,* see Marianne Hirsch, *Family Frames: Photography, Narrative, and Postmemory* (Cambridge: Harvard University Press, 1997), pp. 177–84.

NOTES TO CHAPTER FIVE

1. For a range of suggestive and insightful analyses of the Thomas nomination and hearings, see Toni Morrison, ed., *Race-ing Justice, En-gendering Power: Essays on Anita Hill, Clarence Thomas, and the Construction of Social Reality* (New York: Pantheon, 1992).

2. Robert Gooding-Williams, "Introduction," in *Reading Rodney King Reading Urban Uprising,* ed. Robert Gooding-Williams (New York: Routledge, 1993), p. 1.

3. The works I have in mind include, but are not limited to: Ann duCille, *Skin Trade* (Cambridge: Harvard University Press, 1996); Darnell M. Hunt, *Screening the Los Angeles "Riots:" Race, Seeing, and Resistance* (New York: Cambridge University Press, 1997); Toni Morrison, ed., *Race-ing Justice, En-gendering Power;* Toni Morrison and Claudia Brodsky Lacour, ed., *Birth of a Nation'hood: Gaze, Script, and Spectacle in the O. J. Simpson Case* (New York: Pantheon, 1997); Patricia J. Williams, *The Rooster's Egg: On the Persistence of Prejudice* (Cambridge: Harvard University Press, 1995); Robert Gooding-Williams, ed., *Reading Rodney King Reading Urban Uprising* (New York: Routledge, 1993).

4. Haile Gerima, "Thoughts and Concepts: The Making of *Ashes and Embers,*" *Black American Literature Forum* 25. 2 (Summer 1991): 335.

5. Ibid., p. 349.

6. Clyde Taylor, "Decolonizing the Image: New U. S. Black Cinema," *Jump Cut,* ed., Peter Steven (New York: Praeger, 1985), p. 168.

7. Ibid.

8. For an especially rich discussion of *Bush Mama,* see Mike Murashige, "Haile Gerima and the Political Economy of Cinematic Resistance," in *Representing Blackness: Issues in Film and Video,* ed. Valerie Smith (New Brunswick, NJ: Rutgers University Press, 1997) pp. 183–203.

9. See Jerry G. Watts, insightful analysis of the shock many African

NOTES TO CHAPTER FIVE

Americans and progressive whites experienced upon hearing the verdicts in this trial in his essay, "Reflections on the Rodney King Verdict and the Paradoxes of the Black Response," in *Reading Rodney King Reading Urban Uprising,* pp. 236–48.

10. As Jerry G. Watts has written: "An important telltale of the escapist ethos of large sectors of poor black Americans lies in the fact that the recent rioting in Los Angeles did not begin immediately following the airing of the video film of the Rodney King beating over Los Angeles television. Would-be rioters waited under the hope that American justice, whatever that is, would prevail." See "Reflections on the Rodney King Verdict and the paradoxes of the Black Response" in *Reading Rodney King Reading Urban Uprising,* p. 240.

11. As Andrew Goodwin notes, "[The King video clip] put left and radical critics of the media in a strange dilemma; having argued for more than a decade that media analysis shows the partial and manipulated nature of media representations, some now took the contrary position—that the clip was essentially "true." See his "Truth, Justice and Videotape," *Inside the L. A. Riots: What Really Happened—and Why It Will Happen Again,* ed., Institute for Alternative Journalism (New York, 1992), p. 122.

12. Judith Butler, "Endangered/Endangering: Schematic Racism and White Paranoia," in *Reading Rodney King Reading Urban Uprising,* p. 17.

13. As Kimberlé Crenshaw and Gary Peller argue in their insightful analysis of the implications of this defense strategy: "The videotape images were *physically* mediated by the illustration board upon which the still pictures were mounted, and in the same moment of *disaggregation,* they were *symbolically* mediated by the new narrative backdrops of the technical discourse of institutional security and the reframing of King as a threat rather than a victim." See "Reel Time/Real Justice," in *Reading Rodney King Reading Urban Uprising,* p. 59.

NOTES TO CHAPTER FIVE

14. For instance, the coverage brought into focus the differential status of U.S.-born Chicanas and Chicanos and recent Central American immigrants, class distinctions among African Americans, and the disparate economic positions of Korean, Japanese, and Chinese immigrants, distinctions that categories such as Latina/o, African American, or Asian American generally conceal.

15. For divergent responses to the place of experience in the classroom, see Diana Fuss, *Essentially Speaking: Feminism, Nature and Difference* (New York: Routledge, 1989) and bell hooks, "Essentialism and Experience," *American Literary History* 3 (Spring 1991): 172–83.

16. Cherly I. Harris, "Whiteness as Property," Harvard Law Review 106 (June 1993): 1768–69.

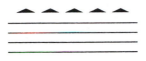

Index

▲ ▲ ▲ ▲